Childfree After Infertility

Childfree After Infertility

✦

Moving From Childlessness to a Joyous Life

Heather Wardell

iUniverse, Inc.
New York Lincoln Shanghai

Childfree After Infertility
Moving From Childlessness to a Joyous Life

iUniverse, Inc.

For information address:
iUniverse, Inc.
2021 Pine Lake Road, Suite 100
Lincoln, NE 68512
www.iuniverse.com

ISBN: 0-595-27438-2

Printed in the United States of America

For the many wonderful people who were willing to give me their stories, often in very painful detail, to help others move through infertility.

For Wes, for his constant support and encouragement through infertility, career changes, and writer's block.

For my family, for their love, help, and support throughout my infertility and into my new life.

And in memory of Kent, a wonderful cousin taken much too soon, and an inspiration.

Contents

Introduction xi

CHAPTER 1   Welcome To The Journey 1
- *What This Book Is About* *2*

CHAPTER 2   Living With Infertility 4
- *What Infertility Is Like* *4*
    Physical *5*
    Emotional *6*
    Mental *8*
    Spiritual *9*
- *Family And Friends* *9*
- *Deciding To Move On* *11*

CHAPTER 3   Childless Versus Childfree: What Is The
             Difference? 14

CHAPTER 4   Choosing To Be Childfree: WHAT Choice? 19

CHAPTER 5   How Do You Become Childfree? 23

CHAPTER 6   What Will The Childfree Life Be Like? 27
- *What Will Happen When You Grow Old?* *33*

CHAPTER 7   "Why Don't You Just Adopt?": Dealing With
             Others 36
- *Strangers and Acquaintances* *37*
- *Friends* *39*
- *Family* *42*

CHAPTER 8   The Journey Continues 46

APPENDIX A   Resources For The Childfree Lifestyle 49

APPENDIX B   Stories 55

APPENDIX C   References 69

Acknowledgements

I am so very grateful to the many wonderful people who responded to my call for stories and sent me the details of their painful experiences with infertility. While they were incredibly difficult to read at times, due to the memories that they called up for me, they have made this book, and I am so honoured that they chose to share their lives with me. It's a long list of names, but I wouldn't feel right about leaving anyone out!

Adrienne, Amber, Angela, Anne, Beatriz, Cherry, Colleen, Deanna, Diane, Elise, Elizabeth, Ellen, Elma, Erin, Hilary, Janine, Jeanna, Jenn, Jennifer, Joyce, Katherine, Kirsten, Kit, Laurie, Lisa, Marcy, Mary, Maryrose, Meg, Mel, Nancy, Nellie, Petra, Rachel, Roxanne, Rhonda, Robin, Ruth, Sally, Sarah, Sherry, Sissy, Sue, Susan, Tammy, Tyra, Wanda, and anyone else that I might have missed, thank you so much for your generosity and helpfulness.

I am also extremely thankful for the ladies of Bairnsaor. I would still be mired in childlessness were it not for you. Cathleen, Christie, Kit, Laurie, Lisa, Lynda, Norma, Pam, Susan, Tammy, Wendy, and of course Joyce, for creating both the list and the first web site I ever found on becoming childfree after infertility. I owe you all so much!

Introduction

Infertility affects one in ten people of reproductive age—6.1 million people a year in the United States alone. Infertility organizations estimate that just over 50% of these people eventually do go on to conceive and have a child. But what of the millions who do not?

While some certainly choose to adopt a child, many are left childless. Prevented from achieving what seems so effortless for others, their lives become deeply painful. Many are caught in the seemingly endless cycle of increasingly invasive procedures and humiliating inspections of their most intimate lives.

Anger, pain, frustration, and depression result. Relationships are often irreparably damaged by these emotions, and by frequent feelings of guilt, blame, and resentment. 'Giving up' and stopping treatment feels like failure, and they often fear what their lives will be like if they 'resign' themselves to not having children.

But 'giving up' is not the only option, and you do not have to 'resign' yourself to a childless existence. There is another way out of infertility. It is a way that does not include having a child of your own, but does include having a full and happy life, and choosing to live it to the utmost.

The many people who spoke to me for this book are in various stages of reaching this lofty goal. Some are now completely childfree, and live happy and fulfilling lives. Others can see the light at the end of the tunnel, but have not yet reached it. Others are still mired in the depths of infertility, and cannot fathom life without a child of their own. No matter where you currently fit into this continuum, you too can find a rich and meaningful life without children.

All of the stories that I have used within this book are true. In all cases, I have assigned new names to the people involved, and changed identifying details where necessary. Not everyone is comfortable being completely open with their most intimate details, and I wanted to be sure that my participants felt free to express what they had experienced without fear of being exposed.

I wish you all the best in your journey from infertility to a joyous childfree life. I know first-hand how difficult it can be, and how hard it can be to imagine a new way of life. But there *is* a new way of life waiting for you, and it can be better than you could ever have dreamed.

1

Welcome To The Journey

"Watch the baby while I gather up her stuff, OK?" I nodded, and Angela disappeared into the bathroom. Maggie, less than three weeks old, lay quietly on the change table looking up at me. I couldn't believe how small she was, how fragile she seemed. Almost before I realized I was doing it, I scooped her up into my arms and held her against my shoulder.

She was just as delicate as she had appeared, so light that I could hardly feel her in my arms. She smelled clean and fresh, and her skin was incredibly soft. It was so hard for me to wrap my mind around the fact that this tiny child had been created by my two good friends from university, that she was a *part* of both of them and would not have existed without them.

Memories of my year of infertility flashed through my mind. I remembered the desperate longing for a child, the deep despair every month when I realized that I had 'failed' yet again, and the agony of seeing other people pregnant or with babies. I had been so certain that a life without children would not be worth living, that the only true success would be creating a child with my husband, that nothing else mattered.

I leaned Maggie back slightly so that I could look at her tiny face, and thought, "If things had worked out the way I had originally planned, I would have had one just like you." I waited for the old feelings of pain and anger, but they did not come. Instead, my next thought was, "I'm so glad it didn't happen."

My husband and I tried to have a baby throughout 1998, and my constant cycles of increasing anticipation and sudden despair nearly destroyed our marriage. I was so obsessed with having a baby that I hated every pregnant woman I saw. I felt that there were a set number of babies available to be born, and each pregnant woman had 'taken' mine away from me. Even though I knew it wasn't true, I couldn't stop feeling the fury.

All of my memories of that year are dark and painful. Remembering it makes me feel like I'm sinking into a deep pit filled with icy water.

Nearly five years later, my life is now happy, rich, and full, and I am genuinely glad both that we do not have children *and* that I went through such a difficult experience. I am so much stronger now as a result. How did I move from such pain and obsession to being honestly happy that we did not have a child? This book is about the process.

Anyone who has lived with infertility knows the pain, anger, frustration, guilt, and envy that can overwhelm you at a moment's notice. I am here to tell you that it is possible to escape the cycle, and to *choose* to be happily childfree. Many of the people who shared their stories with me for this book have told me that they no longer even *consider* themselves to be infertile, because they have moved on. While you might not yet be comfortable moving that far away from your infertility, you may well be ready to consider moving on into a happier life. It can be a difficult journey, but it is well worth the trip.

WHAT THIS BOOK IS ABOUT

In late 1998, my husband and I decided to take a year off from trying to have a baby, after the stress and pain became too much for me. We never went back, choosing instead to be childfree. I will not try to tell you that it was always an easy process; it most certainly was not. There was a lot of soul-searching required, a lot of examination of our deepest, previously unexamined, reasons for wanting a child. For the most part, it was work that we did on our own, without resources to guide us.

When I first began to consider stopping trying for a baby, I tried to find books and information on how this could be done. The many infertility books that I read either contained nothing on people who had decided to stop trying, or they included one or two paragraphs, near the end of the book, about people who had 'given up'. This was definitely not the help I needed.

I eventually turned to the Internet, and was able there to find people who had chosen to be childfree. Some of these people had decided at a very young age that they would not have children, and were very happy. At the time, though, I didn't feel as though I had any choice in the matter at all. I was infertile, and that was why I didn't have kids. No choice at all.

I spent a few months on a mailing list for the childfree by choice, but eventually left because many of the members were far more militantly childfree (and, in some cases, anti-child) than I was. I do believe that they have every right to feel that way; however, I was beginning to hate children, and that was not what I wanted for myself. These people did give me the idea that it was possible to choose not to have children, which I had truly never considered before, and I am grateful for that.

But I don't hate children, and I knew I still wanted to have them in my life, in some way. I searched for information that would help me. I did eventually find one web site for the childfree after infertility, and soon started my own site describing the changes in my life. I have received hundreds of email messages thanking me for my site, for telling people that it is perfectly fine to both like children *and* choose not to have them, that it is acceptable to have been infertile and to *choose* to stop treatments. I am thrilled to have been able to provide this support, and this book will extend it to even more people.

Many of the people I speak to have moved on from infertility, and now consider themselves to be happily childfree. Many, unfortunately, still consider themselves to be infertile, to have something missing from their lives, to be childless. This book is for them.

I intend to help you understand what it means to live 'childfree', and why it is *not* the same as living 'childless'. It *is* possible for an infertile person to *choose* not to have children, and I will explain how this can happen. As well, I will explain how you can truly label yourself as 'formerly infertile', and how you can be honestly happy for a friend with a new baby without feeling envious.

I know that living childfree is not for everyone. At the end of the next chapter, you will find some questions and exercises to help you decide whether it might be for you. Later chapters will explain how other people have made the choice, and will discuss possible roadblocks along the way. An entire chapter deals with the comments that you may receive from friends and family, and how you might choose to respond.

I will not be discussing any infertility treatment processes in this book, nor will I be covering methods to become permanently childfree. There are other books available for the latter, and, if you choose to become childfree, you will not need the former.

I know first-hand the nearly unbearable pain and confusion that infertility can bring, and I also know the peace and joy that choosing to live your life on your own terms gives. My hope for every reader is that you will be able to decide whether living childfree is for you, and if it is, that you will have the kind of joyous life that I have found.

2

Living With Infertility

The title of this chapter may have surprised you. "Why am I reading about infertility in a book about how to escape it?" There are two main reasons for this.

I want this book to also be useful to counsellors, doctors, and other people who might not have personally experienced infertility. Unfortunately, some of the professionals who work with infertile people do not truly understand what it is like, and the impact that it can have. I hope that, through this chapter, these people may come to know more about infertility's effects.

As well, infertility has a way of making people feel alone. It is rarely discussed, and many people experiencing it find that they do not know anyone else who is going through the same thing. While everyone does experience it differently, there are certain things that are essentially universal. I found it helpful to realize that I wasn't alone while going through infertility, and that I wasn't alone in investigating the childfree lifestyle after infertility. Neither are you.

WHAT INFERTILITY IS LIKE

Infertility has a dramatic impact on nearly all areas of life. It generally becomes harder to deal with, and more demanding, as time goes on. As you see more and more of your friends and family having children, seemingly without any problems, maybe without even intending to do so, it becomes increasingly more difficult to greet their 'happy' news with a smile.

Naturally, different people experience it in different ways. I, for example, was sad at times during my attempts for a baby, but was far more often blazingly angry. Other people, in contrast, feel guilty for not providing their spouse or parents with a child, or feel cheated out of something.

All areas of life are interrelated, and so it is not surprising that infertility's effects are far-reaching. The discussion below will break these effects down into physical, mental, emotional, and spiritual ones.

Physical

For most people, making love is an important part of their marriage. Nearly everyone expects to become pregnant very quickly, without having to do anything 'unusual' in the bedroom. You know that it can take a few months to become pregnant, but you generally do not believe that it will take *you* this long. Terry said, "We figured when we were ready to have a baby, we would 'try,' conceive, and have a baby. Just like that. Little did we know."

After what seems like a reasonable amount of time has passed, you may begin taking your temperature first thing in the morning to determine whether you're ovulating, and if so, when. This leads directly into careful timing of sex (and agonizing over exactly when it should happen). This, naturally, does not do wonders for your sex life.

If these methods alone are not sufficient, you may move into a medical assessment. The emotional impact of this will be discussed below, but there can be a substantial physical impact as well. Generally, the woman undergoes most of the tests, which may range from ultrasound to exploratory surgery under full anesthetic. Helen told me, "Along with the monthly blood checks, there were monthly intrauterine ultrasounds. It was really embarrassing because the device looked like a vibrator. They even covered it with a rubber!"

With any luck, your doctor is compassionate, understanding, and supportive. Unfortunately, that is not always the case. Rose said, "The specialist was awful. I really hated him. In our first meeting with him he lectured us on the expense of having a child. He told us we would need at least a half-million dollars to raise a child. Both my husband and I were university educated people with professional jobs and this man treated us as if we were idiots." While it is appropriate to make sure that prospective patients understand both the costs and the likelihood of successful treatment, this can most certainly be done without belittling the couple.

Amber's doctor reached new lows in bedside manner and compassion. Amber and her husband were in the office for a post-coital test. They had made love in the morning, and now the doctor would check to see whether the sperm were alive and swimming properly. Amber's husband, at the doctor's request, had had a sperm test done two weeks before. The doctor took the sample from Amber, and called the couple into his office while he examined it. He stared into his microscope for what seemed like an eternity, and then asked the husband if he had had a sperm test. He said that he had, and the doctor said, "Hmmm," and continued to stare into his microscope. Amber told me, "My heart just stopped beating. All we could do was stare at each other in shock." The doctor eventually said, in a very offhand manner, "Yeah, everything's fine." Infertility is certainly more than difficult enough without feeling that your doctors are unfeeling and cold.

Fertility drugs, if needed, may cause a wide variety of different side effects. I spent three months on Clomid (a milder ovulation stimulator), experiencing severe hot flashes and mood swings. Samantha also took Clomid, and told me that "nothing except out-of-control emotions came from that". These and other side effects only serve to remind you over and over of what you are trying to do, and that it isn't working. As well, you do run the risk of a multiple pregnancy, which not everyone is truly prepared for. I was able to imagine having twins or even triplets, but the idea of a larger order pregnancy terrified me, and so I did not move on to any of the stronger medications.

In vitro fertilization and artificial insemination procedures are deeply invasive, and stunningly expensive to boot. While my husband and I chose not to go this route, it is clear to me that the physical impact, while substantial, may actually be less difficult to handle than the emotional effects.

Having a baby is 'supposed' to be something natural and easy, an expression of your love for each other. Infertility changes it into a strongly medical situation, in which you lose your control of your life, love, and emotions. For me, and for many of the people who shared their stories with me, it was this loss of control that led to the devastating emotional, mental, and spiritual impacts of infertility.

Emotional

Most women believe that they will become pregnant just as easily as their friends and family members do. When this does not happen, it can be absolutely devastating. Hilary told me that she felt like "a freak of nature", and "unnatural because everything reproduces, even the weeds".

Among the many emotions that occur (often at the same time, and often in contradictory ways) are:

- Feeling betrayed by your body

- Feeling cheated out of something that 'should' have been easy

- Furious anger at those who conceive easily or are pregnant

- Guilt for any real or perceived past 'bad behaviour' that caused your infertility

- Anger that your spouse is not as upset about the infertility as you are

- Anger that he or she *is* as upset, and therefore cannot support you effectively

- Desperate belief that the next treatment will work, no matter how unlikely it truly is

- Belief that you truly will never be pregnant (often accompanied by strong guilt and a feeling that you are causing the infertility by this belief)

- Terror of being childless for ever, and of having a horrible life as a result

- Dramatic mood swings between any and all of the above feelings and beliefs

One of the saddest parts of infertility is the silence surrounding it. Many people choose to tell only a very few people about their situation. This is an understandable thing to do, as telling too many people can make things even more painful as everyone waits with varying degrees of patience to hear good news. Unfortunately, not telling can also cause incredibly difficult emotional situations.

During my infertility, I worked with a man whose wife had become pregnant accidentally. He spent what seemed like hours bemoaning his fate to everyone. I was furious with him for this, furious with myself for being angry at him when he did not know what I was going through, and deeply bitter that he and his wife had achieved accidentally what I could not do with tremendous effort. To top it off, I also felt incredibly guilty about all of my anger towards him. Given this stew of emotions, is it any wonder that the most painful thing to hear is, "Just relax and you'll get pregnant!"? I have yet to hear from anyone who actually found such a statement comforting.

In a time when much of your control is being taken away, it may begin to feel appropriate to lash out at others who have managed to achieve what you cannot. I remember walking into the train station on my way home from work, and seeing a pregnant woman eating a chocolate chip cookie. I don't remember her face; I only remember the bulge of her belly, and my overwhelming fury. How dare she endanger her baby by eating that way? It was all I could do to keep from snatching the cookie away from her. Many of the people I surveyed shared similar experiences. Of course, I knew that this was completely irrational. Far from helping me, though, that knowledge just made me feel worse.

The impact on your marriage can also be substantial. As I mentioned above, there can be tremendous anger and guilt between spouses as a result of infertility. If it is known which of the partners' bodies is the one with the problems, that person may feel terribly guilty about 'robbing' their partner of a child, while the other partner may feel badly for still wanting a child despite the difficulties. If the cause of your infertility is unknown, both partners may feel the guilt and the sadness at the same time. Sometimes, one partner refuses to be tested, for fear that the problem will damage their sense of masculinity or femininity.

Some people have found that the experience of having gone through infertility together actually leaves the marriage stronger as a result. This has certainly been my experience. Wes and I made it through together, by working together to learn to support each other, and I can honestly say that our lives have never been richer or more complete.

During the infertility itself, however, the situation was very different. I was angry with him for not being as upset as I was, and felt very much alone. I felt that if we did not have a child, we would not have anything to live for, and I was upset that he could see a life for us without children.

I myself had not really given any thought to there being any other life plan for me besides the 'traditional' one of motherhood. Part of why my infertility produced such anger in me was that I felt blocked on the path, for no apparent reason. I'd been a 'good girl' and done what I was supposed to, and yet the reward wasn't forthcoming! I was furiously angry, and felt cheated.

Emma described the emotional impact of infertility very clearly. "This has been a really difficult emotional struggle. The cycle of hope and disappointment has been like a rollercoaster ride. Although, so far, I don't dare get off in case that the opportunity of becoming pregnant is waiting just around the next turn or corkscrew or over the next hill. On top of that, having so many hormones because of the medications, I am never quite sure the extent that my feelings are authentic and the amount that the medication is affecting me."

Mental

Even at the time, I was very much aware that my fury at the pregnant woman eating the cookie was completely unreasonable and irrational. This knowledge, however, did not stop me feeling this way. It can be very difficult to feel these sorts of illogical emotions, knowing that they don't make sense, and yet to find yourself unable to stop them.

It is very common to find yourself blaming pregnant women for having taken *your* baby. Even though you know that it isn't true, it can be very difficult to shake off the belief. In my darkest moments, I even entertained thoughts of snatching another woman's baby and running away with it.

You may also become obsessed with thoughts of having a child, and find that your entire life revolves around it. Conversely, you may find yourself completely convinced that you will never have a child. Or, like me, you might manage to combine both into one.

I never once truly believed and accepted that I could get pregnant and have a baby, and I went through a lot of guilt as a result, wondering whether it was my own lack of faith that prevented me from having one.

In your darkest moments, you may try to imagine life without a child, and see nothing but a wasted life. I was convinced that there would be nothing good in my life if I did not have a child, that being a mother was the only worthwhile path.

These constant thoughts can leave you with even more stress and frustration than you had before. It is a vicious circle, and leads to infertility consuming your life.

Spiritual

Infertility can have a strong impact on spirituality. Some people find that their faith is strengthened by the situation, and feel very strongly that they are being put through this for a reason. Others find their faith shaken instead, and may feel as though their baby is being 'withheld' from them because of something they did or did not do.

People who did not have strong religious beliefs prior to their infertility may find themselves turning to some higher power for support during the difficult times. Others may instead see their situation as proof that there is no higher power (or, at any rate, no higher power that is taking care of them).

FAMILY AND FRIENDS

The vast majority of people going through infertility tell only a very few of their friends and family members about their situation. There are many different reasons for this.

Some people feel embarrassed about their infertility. Fertility is so tied into sex, which is rarely talked about among family or friends, that it can feel deeply embarrassing to discuss something that many people will see as 'problems in the bedroom'.

Other people see their infertility as their own business, and not something to be discussed with the world at large. I shared this view (and, to some extent, still do). However, it does make it very difficult for your friends and family to be able to empathize with you, and they may inadvertently make insensitive comments.

Yet another reason not to share your infertility problems with all and sundry is that some people are incredibly insensitive even when they *do* know about your situation. Comments such as, "Gee, my husband just has to look at me and I get pregnant", "Just relax and you'll get pregnant", or "Why don't you just adopt?" are, unfortunately, all too common. I was careful to only share my situation with people who I thought would be able to understand and support me, at least to some degree, and even so, I received some of these sorts of comments. They leave you feeling even more abnormal and alone than you felt before.

Other people will genuinely want to say the right thing, but will not know what that thing is. Society is organized around the idea that people grow up, get married, buy a nice house, and have children, and many people have honestly never considered the possibility of there being another option. Your infertility is outside of their experience, and they simply do not know how to deal with it. It is not surprising that they do not always manage to find the right thing to say or do.

These people might make comments about being sure that you will get pregnant eventually, and that maybe you should see a different doctor. Even though they are trying to be kind and helpful, their comments may only make you feel more like a failure, and like you are doing something wrong.

Your own parents tend to be the ones who have the most difficulty with your infertility. The vast majority of parents have been anticipating grandchildren someday, and your infertility threatens that dream. Just as you have to adjust your expectations of your life as you go through infertility and come out the other side, they must do so as well.

However, you do have some choice in the matter; you can choose to continue treatments, or to adopt, or to live childfree. They, however, must accept what you give or do not give to them. Of course, this is as it should be, but it can be very difficult for your parents to accept. Chapter 7 discusses family issues in more detail.

DECIDING TO MOVE ON

As we have seen, infertility can have incredibly far-reaching effects, disrupting not only your entire life but also the lives of your family and friends. As the months and even years go by, the wider its reach can become.

How, though, do you decide when you have had enough? How do you know when it is time for you to stop trying to have a baby and start living again? This is a very personal decision. Many people say that they just 'knew' when it was time to stop. That was certainly my experience.

Right after I had been scheduled to have exploratory surgery to see whether my ovaries were working properly, Wes and I were at the mall, and two women went by with small children in strollers. I burst into tears, and couldn't stop. Wes had to guide me out of the mall and take me home.

I remember sitting curled up in a chair, with our black cat snuggling up to me trying to comfort me, and saying over and over, "I can't do this any more, I can't." I closed my eyes and tried to imagine how it would be to keep trying, and it was terrible. I then tried to imagine 'taking a break' (I wasn't ready to imagine stopping completely), and I felt so totally peaceful and relaxed immediately. I just knew that I needed the break. We never went back. While I do occasionally feel twinges for 'what might have been', I know that we made the right decision.

When I asked Cathy how she knew that she was ready to stop trying, she told me, "I guess I knew when I'd had a procedure done by a doctor, and I just didn't care to get the results. I never did. It just didn't matter anymore." Katherine's story was even more dramatic. I have quoted her below, as her words are so powerful.

"Then it hit me. I'm not sure of when it hit me. That was a shame, as I would have loved to know a date.

I remember where I was though. I know exactly at what corner and at what light I was sitting. I was in my now defunct 1990 Nissan Sentra four-door sedan when this revelation hit. It was mid-morning on a winter's day, probably in February of 1997.

I heard a voice inside my head tell me, "You're too young to be feeling this way. You know that whether or not you conceive does not make any difference in the kind of woman you are. How much longer are you going to let this ruin your days?"

That was it. I never looked back. Never felt bad or guilty. It was as if someone had turned on a light. No more pain and no more crying.

I had my life back again."

For some people, the realization that you are no longer willing and able to keep trying for a baby does come as suddenly and clearly as it did for Cathy, Katherine, and me. For others, though, it is hard to determine when you need to move on. Here are some questions to think about. There are no right or wrong answers; these are only to give you a framework for your thinking. If possible, you and your partner should both answer these questions individually, and then discuss your responses. Where your answers are different, talk about it and try to understand the other viewpoint. Do not try to change the other person's mind; it is so important that you each have the right to feel the way that you feel.

The questions that ask you to rate something are based on a scale from one to ten, where 'one' is 'not at all' and 'ten' is 'the most possible'. The rest are for you to think about and discuss with your partner. Be completely honest with yourself and with each other; it can be painful but it is necessary if you truly want to make the right decision for you.

1. Rate how much you want to have a child.

2. Rate how much you think your partner wants to have a child.

3. What do you imagine that your child would be like?

4. Rate how accurate and realistic you think your response to question #3 is.

5. Imagine yourself as a parent. Can you see yourself with a newborn? A toddler? A school-age child? A teenager? Take the time to really imagine yourself at each stage, and see what you think it will be like. Try to think of both the good and the bad things about having the child that you are imagining. During my infertility, I could only see the good sides. Immediately after deciding to stop, I could only see the bad. Both sides are there, though, and they deserve equal consideration.

6. Try the exercise that I went through above. Sit quietly, and imagine yourself continuing to try for a baby. How do you feel at the thought of it? Take as much time as you need to truly picture it. What would your days be like? Your evenings? Your job? Your home?

7. When you are finished, imagine stopping infertility treatments. How do you feel at the thought of it? Picture your life. Think about what you would want to do with the rest of your life. Would you change jobs? Move? Volunteer?

Many more things are possible without children; imagine them, and see how you would feel about them.

There are many more questions for your consideration in the book 'The Parenthood Decision' by Beverly Engel. Please look into this book or visit my web site if you are still trying to decide whether you are ready to stop trying for a baby. (There is more information about my web site and about 'The Parenthood Decision' in Appendix A.)

Do also pay attention to your daily thoughts and feelings about your life. Nicole said, "I knew it was time to stop trying when trying took over our lives. I found I started being angry with my husband for not wanting to have sex at the precise moment we were supposed to. The conversation would go something like, 'But it's four o'clock on Tuesday, I don't care if you don't feel like it, we have to do it now!'. I got to a point when I started to wonder if it was worth killing each other for, and after a while I realised we were happy just the way we were." No sudden lightning bolt, just a dawning recognition that life could be great without a child.

If, after you have answered and truly considered these questions, you feel certain that you and your partner still want a child enough to keep trying, then that is wonderful. It is possible that simply having clarified your feelings will help you conceive; even if it does not, you will be moving ahead knowing for certain that you are doing what is right for you. I wish you all the best!

If, however, you feel instead that you are no longer willing to put yourself through the effort of trying to have a child, if it no longer seems to be what is right for you, then this book is for you. I will show you how you can truly choose to live a life without children, and how it can be absolutely wonderful.

One caution, though. Do not assume that you will never feel sad about not having had a child, or that you will never feel that you are missing out on something. You most likely will feel both of these things from time to time. I certainly still do, and I am currently coming up to the fifth year anniversary of my decision to stop trying.

Every choice that we make in life involves *not* choosing something else, and the 'road not taken' can often seem better than the one we're on. If the other path *always* seems better, then perhaps you are on the wrong path. If it is only an occasional feeling, try to see it as simply a recognition that there are good things on the other path. Focus on the many joyful events on your own path, and accept that it's just not possible to have it all.

3

Childless Versus Childfree: What Is The Difference?

At this point in the book, you are probably in one of two frames of mind. You might have decided that you are definitely ready to move on and find a happier life than the one you've been living during your infertility. On the other hand, you might still be not quite sure that the childfree lifestyle is really for you.

In either case, it is a difficult and painful thing to stop striving for a dream that you may have been working toward for many years. Be sure to take care of yourself as you move through this book and through the process of becoming childfree. Share your thoughts and feelings only with those people who will genuinely support you in what you choose to do.

More and more articles are being written on the subject of choosing not to have children. They usually use the term 'childless' to refer to people without children. The word 'childfree' has developed something of a stigma, and is seen as referring to people who hate children, or who are too self-absorbed and fussy to be bothered with children.

I think it's unfortunate that this has happened, because there is a very real difference between describing yourself as 'childless' and being 'childfree', and both terms are necessary. Neither should be a judgement call; they are both a description of a certain place in life.

To be 'childless' is to be without a child and to wish that the situation were otherwise. When you are in the midst of infertility, you are nearly always in a childless state of mind. When you see children, you wish that they were yours. You are angry and bitter sometimes, and deeply sad at other times, about not being able to have a child, and you are focused (sometimes to the exclusion of all else) on the desire to have a child.

Your life may begin to revolve around having a child, and the focus of your marriage often completely shifts as well. Any other interests that you have may be

14

set aside in the pursuit of pregnancy, and all of your energy goes toward trying to have a baby. You feel a distinct lack in your life, and are trying to fill it. Childlessness also involves a feeling of not having control over events; you want a child, but are being prevented from having one through no fault of your own.

Margaret, in the midst of infertility and having suffered through repeated miscarriages, told me, "I'm tired of wanting a child of my own for so long… tired of injections, medications, the heartache and the failures… I live my life dragging a burden on my soul." These are the feelings of childlessness.

To be childfree, on the other hand, is also to be without a child. However, the truly childfree person is genuinely happy with life as it stands, and does not feel a lack because there is no child. You have chosen not to have children, and have many other things in your life. Since you have made the choice, you do have control over your life and its events.

You may be thinking, "That's all very well for people who did *choose* not to have kids, but I didn't! I wanted them and couldn't have them!" This is true to a degree, but I believe that it will have a substantial negative impact on your life if you continue to think this way.

Yes, infertility took away your ability to have a child as easily as your friends and family can, and that was certainly not your choice. However, you *do* have choices in this. You have the choice of what treatments you will have, and for how long you will continue them. You can decide whether you will pursue adoption. You, also, have the choice to stop the process and learn to live childfree.

Please do not think of this as being second best. Just as an adopted child is not somehow less than a biological one, so the childfree lifestyle is not less than parenthood. It is different. It can be hard to imagine, and I found it incredibly difficult at first, but your life can actually be better as a childfree person than as a parent. It is all up to you, and how you choose to handle and organize your life.

My dear online friend Joyce, the owner of the first web site I found about being childfree after infertility, described it this way:

"Frequently, people will say that we got lemons in life and we are making lemonade. That is a very sweet sentiment. However, I disagree with it. Life did not give us lemons. Our lives were lemonade to begin with. We thought that we might like the lemonade a little sweeter. We just couldn't get the extra sugar in the drink. We took a second sip and decided that our lemonade was perfect just as it is. That's not giving up—it's appreciating what you already have."

Many women have told me that they no longer even consider themselves infertile, even though they may have multiple fertility problems. They have chosen to move on from infertility and live happy childfree lives, and infertility is no longer part of their lives. Some call themselves 'formerly infertile', and some do not consider it even important enough for that label any more.

I love having cats, and I would feel very sad if I no longer had any cats in my home and in my life. If they were suddenly gone, I would be 'catless'. On the other hand, while I also love dogs and grew up with golden retrievers, I do not have a dog of my own. I enjoy dogs, and enjoy spending time with my parents' dogs, but I have no interest in rearranging my life to make it suitable for a dog. Without a cat, I would be *catless*. Without a dog, I am *dogfree*. It is more than just terminology; it is a mindset and a way of seeing your life.

Please note that I am not suggesting that you deny your feelings, and pretend that you never really wanted a child. All this will do is leave you feeling even more upset and frustrated. What I am suggesting is that you continue to think long and hard about how you want your life to be, and work on imagining what it could be without children.

Very few people have told me that they simply woke up one morning and realized that they had become childfree. It usually takes a lot of time to move from infertility to the childfree point of view, and even then, it is not usually a one-time decision.

I stopped trying to have a baby in 1998, and still occasionally get pangs of wishing that things were different, and wanting to have a child right now. When they happen, though, I have learned to examine what is going on in my life. I thought long and hard about choosing to be childfree, and I know it the right decision for me. I have found that my occasional changes of desire are always related to one of two things.

One of my recent feelings of, "I really want a baby" came the day that I spent three hours with the vice-principal at my new school, my first teaching position. He went very quickly through everything that I would need to teach, much of which I did not know well enough to teach. I left the school, my mind spinning with all that I had to learn, remember, and be able to teach, and went to the mall to window-shop. I walked past a maternity store, and immediately had to fight off tears, as I 'realized' that I had made a huge mistake and was definitely meant to have children.

I sat down on a nearby bench and forced myself to think it all through. It eventually became very clear to me that I was afraid of all that I would have to learn and be able to do at my new school, and that I wanted to hide myself away.

The ironic thing is that having a child of my own would have been far more difficult and scary than learning to teach, and yet it somehow seems to feel like the best alternative.

I think that this happens because 'everybody' has children, and so nearly everyone understands what new parents are going through. People see them as needing support and encouragement, and it is usually cheerfully provided. I felt a desperate need for that kind of encouragement, and on some level only felt that I could get it by having a baby.

Once I realized what was happening, I went home and reviewed the material that I needed to teach. When I had it fairly clearly figured out in my mind, the 'need' for a baby dissipated.

Another recent one, of which I am not terribly proud, came after the christening of a friend's baby. Their home was full of friends and family, all so proud of them, and I left in tears. A large part of my desire for children was a need to fit in, and to have people be proud of me, and it hurt to see them receiving what I had wanted. I was genuinely happy for them, and I knew that it was not truly what I wanted, but it was still painful to see.

Choosing to be childfree is really a journey, not a destination. You too will have some days where you feel completely childfree and completely happy, and other days where you feel as though you're right back into the worst emotions of your infertility.

Some of the worst times will be holidays (especially those that often revolve around children and family), birthdays and other family gatherings, and anniversaries of significant days of your infertility (such as the date of a miscarriage). Sandra said, "This holiday season has been more difficult than either of us realized it would be. Although we were prepared to not have any company for the holidays, we have both grieved deeply and our emotions have overwhelmed and taken us by surprise several times."

Allow yourself to do the grieving that you need. Infertility has taken a dream away from you, and it is right and good to grieve for that dream, even if you can see another life ahead of you. There is no time limit on this; if you still feel sad four years later, do not tell yourself that it's time to get over it. There is no such thing. You need to release all of the emotions whenever they arise, or they may well spill out in inappropriate ways.

Nadia, who had four miscarriages, told me, "I feel like people feel sorry for me. Sometimes I wish no one knew what had happened so they wouldn't." I think it's natural and normal to feel badly for someone who has gone through so much. However, feeling sorry for someone implies that you think that the person is missing something important.

I admit that I will miss many things because I do not have children. I will not have that first day of school, first date, graduation, and maybe a wedding to attend. However, there are many things that are not available to parents. They cannot spontaneously go away for a weekend or even for an evening, which is usually much easier for the childfree. Parents have worries and fears that we will never have to deal with. I can choose the direction of my life to a much greater extent than a parent can.

The fact is, every decision in life brings with it compromises. When I chose to leave my job in computer programming and go back to school to be a teacher, I left behind my high salary and the frequent business trips that I loved. I gained, though, a feeling that my work is truly valuable and rewarding, and a way to interact with children without having my own. (Please realize that I am not suggesting that all childfree people should have or need this interaction; for me, it was something that was important.)

Choosing to be childfree does involve compromise, but so does choosing to be a parent. If the decision, on either side, is carefully though out and the benefits and sacrifices are well understood, then the decision is almost sure to end up being the right one.

Some people have told me that they are 'childfree for now', but that they'd be happy to have a child if that happened. Rather than truly being childfree, I see this situation as being more of a 'come what may' attitude. This probably does work well in many cases, but I am not at all sure that something as significant as parenthood should be decided this way.

I believe that the decision to have children should never be made lightly, and that people should always think very seriously before choosing to have them. If you are ready, willing, and able to handle it, they can be a joy. If not, it is unfair to them, to you, and to society to have them 'because everyone does'.

So, you may now be ready to begin thinking of yourself as childfree. If so, you are probably wondering how to do this. You don't magically become childfree, unfortunately. In the next chapter, we will talk about how you can truly choose to live your life a different way.

4

Choosing To Be Childfree: WHAT Choice?

It can be difficult to imagine 'choosing' to be childfree after infertility. The fact that you were infertile seems to make it impossible to choose not to have children; wasn't the choice made for you?

Actually, no. In this situation, as in everything in life, you have the ability to choose how you will react. You can choose to make a conscious decision to move on from being infertile and to find a new and different life for yourself. Or, you can choose to stay where you are, and continue to be childless. (Not making a choice, unfortunately, usually means continuing to be childless.)

Julia experienced this. She told me, "It was only *after* the diagnosis that I started craving children. I had several months of 'but I can't have any! Waaah!', before I realized that what I was really upset about was not having the *choice*. So I sat down, and talked with my husband, and seriously *chose*. And I feel much better now."

Some people choose to remain childless because they still have treatments that they would like to try, and are not yet ready to choose to move on. This, of course, is perfectly understandable and healthy. However, some people remain childless for less appropriate reasons.

I have heard from people who find that their childlessness gets them sympathy and caring from friends and family members, which they do not receive in other ways. Other people use their childlessness as an excuse for any and all things that are not right in their lives. "I would change my job/move/start exercising/go back to school if I weren't so depressed about being childless." This is definitely not healthy.

I believe that we always have the ability to choose our responses, even when the situation seems to be entirely out of our control. Even just choosing to consider moving on seems to bring back a lot of the feelings of control that are taken away by infertility.

Helen told me, "Even in just trying on being childfree, a huge weight was lifted from me. I felt like I had hit my head on the wall, been underwater for so long that it was like coming back into myself for the first time. I finally was sure about something. I was finally back in control of my life."

You can feel this way too. You can get control of your life back. But how?

I believe that the first thing to do is to honestly consider what your infertility has meant to your life, as well as what you had expected to gain by having children. Nobody else needs to know your answers if you choose not to share them, so be completely honest and open with yourself. Dig deeper than the typical answers of "To pass on the family name", "To see part of myself in my child", or "To fix the mistakes that my parents made with me". Truly try to understand why you wanted children, and how you feel now that you do not have them. Also consider how you feel about the possibility of never having a child of your own.

I thought about these sorts of questions when I was considering becoming childfree. I realized that my main reasons for wanting a child involved conformity and attention. I felt that 'everyone' had children, and that I would feel more normal if I did, and would fit in better with others. Not having a child would make me different, and I didn't want to be different.

I also saw the attention given to mothers (especially new mothers), and found myself wanting that as well. I wanted the endless discussions about whose eyes the baby had, whether he looked more like Grandma or Grandpa, and whether she was more or less fussy than I had been as a baby. I wanted the feelings of continuity from one generation to another. I also wanted to make my parents proud of me.

Not having a child, to me, felt as though it would go against all of these things. I would be different, and obviously so. I would have to deal with endless questions about why I did not have children, what was wrong with me, and why I hadn't tried harder to deal with it and have a baby. My parents would be disappointed, and my life would be empty and meaningless.

As well, as I've already said, I was furious that I could not easily have a baby. I had always been able to achieve pretty much everything that I set my mind to, and yet somehow pregnancy was eluding me. It was definitely not fair, and my complete and utter lack of ability to change the situation only made it feel worse.

At the time, all of these feelings were valid, and made perfect sense. I had always expected that I would have children, as I really knew very few adults without children. It just seemed to be part of growing up. The idea of missing out on becoming a 'real' adult was both terrible and terrifying to me.

On the day when I broke down at the mall and had to be brought home, though, I realized deep inside that I could no longer continue with this. Infertility was ripping me apart, destroying my marriage, and taking all of the happiness and joy out of my life.

I forced myself, right then, to really re-examine all of my beliefs and attitudes about parenthood, and to truly consider whether I wanted and needed it enough to continue trying to beat my infertility. I thought about how I'd always believed that my life would be completely empty without a child, and tried to imagine what I would do and what I would be if I weren't a mother.

I felt an infinite number of possibilities rushing at me, a vast number of potential paths opening up before me. I could be and do anything. Many of my possibilities would not be available to me as a parent, because of my strong belief that I should stay home with my child.

I still remember the feeling of peace and calm that came over me as I thought about not continuing to try for a baby. Not being devastated each month at the arrival of my period, not feeling angry and bitter toward every pregnant woman or mother that I saw, not being so obsessed with having a baby that nothing else mattered to me.

I looked up at Wes, and simply said, "I think I'm finished." He hugged me, and told me that we would figure it all out together.

In the nearly five years since that day, I have gone back to university, become an elementary school teacher, returned to playing the clarinet that I abandoned after university, begun sewing more of my clothes, written several articles for various web sites, written this book, learned to belly dance, and lost thirty pounds. Far from being empty, my life is beginning to burst at the seams!

This 'imagination exercise', adapted from my web site, can be very useful in helping you to visualize your life as a potentially childfree person.

Imagine how your life will be. Picture yourself daily with a child. See yourself doing all of the little (and not so little) things that a child needs. Take a month, take two, take six. This is a major, *major* life decision, and should not be rushed. (If you feel that "I have to have a baby *right now*", you are in the grips of what is often called "the baby rabies", and you, more than anyone, *must* take the time to truly think it over!)

When you feel that you have a good handle on this side of it, reverse it. Imagine yourself child*free*. You will never have a child. (Think about whether reading that statement makes you feel sick and scared, or relieved.) Picture yourself daily with no children. What will you do with your life? Will you change careers? Change towns? Change relationships? How will you be?

Once you have really thought about both sides of the equation, see which one feels right to you. I use this technique to make many decisions in my life, and I find that usually one option just somehow 'sits' better with me. I feel more calm and comfortable while considering that option.

If neither one truly feels right at this time, then my experiences suggest that you are either not allowing yourself to truly think through both options or you would be fine either way. When this happens to me in less important decisions, I usually either flip a coin or go with the easiest choice.

If this happens to you while deciding whether or not to have a child, I would very strongly suggest that you take that as a decision not to have one. I do not believe that "well, sure, I could have a kid, I guess" is enough to make you decide to have one. There are many sacrifices and life changes involved in having children and raising them properly, and if you don't really care either way, I think you should choose not to have one.

Since you're still with me at this point in the book, I am assuming that you are thinking that the childfree lifestyle might be for you, and that you are wondering how you can truly become childfree. Chapter 5 discusses this in detail.

5

How Do You Become Childfree?

I do not want to give you the impression that it is a simple matter to decide to be childfree. It can be very difficult indeed. You have wanted to have a child for some time, or your infertility would not have affected you so deeply. Even if you are now ready to stop trying, it is still a big step to move from 'being a parent someday' into 'choosing not to have children'.

Looking at the stories that people have given to me for this book, there seems to be two ways that people come to the decision to be childfree. Both are completely valid, and yet they are quite different.

Some people take a very analytical approach. They think through the good sides and bad sides of having children, and of not having them. They think about what being childless is doing to them and their lives, and about what it would be like to consciously choose to step off the infertility track and regain their own lives.

After thinking through all of the options, and doing a lot of soul searching, they make a conscious decision to leave infertility and childlessness behind. They know that they will be missing out on some things in life by making this decision, but they also know that they will gain many things, not the least of which is a strong sense of control over their lives.

My process was like this. I spent a lot of time thinking through what my life would be like if I continued trying to have a child, and what it would be like if I didn't. While the initial spark of the decision came after my breakdown at the shopping mall, it took me nearly a year to be certain that I had made a decision, and that it was the right one.

Angela's situation was very similar. She told me, "I don't think there was any one 'moment' when we knew it was time to stop trying. It's just that after all of the surgery and other invasive medical procedures and years on an emotional roller coaster with no success, it just didn't seem sane to keep it up any more. I got to a point at which I knew I could not take one more month of hope followed by despair. I wanted my life back. I wanted to stop getting up at the crack of dawn every day to monitor my temperature and take urine samples. I wanted sex to stop being a household chore and a means to an end. Finally, we decided together that life should not center on the one thing we could not accomplish, and eventually, we focused on other goals that were achievable. Eventually, I found goals that were not only achievable but added meaning to my life. In other words, it was not so much a moment as a process."

Other people describe becoming childfree after infertility as 'being struck by lightning'. Something happens that suddenly almost seems to make the decision for them. They were infertile and childless, and then, in the next moment, they are childfree.

Katherine, whose story was included in Chapter 2, describes this perfectly. "I was driving my car and it hit me like a lightning bolt. I actually got very angry with myself for wasting my time being depressed and crying. I was too young to feel this way and this kid thing was ruining my days. I swore I would never let it ruin my days ever, and it hasn't." I am privileged to be a good online friend of Katherine's, and I can attest that she has a wonderful life, and has certainly not allowed her infertility to ruin her days.

Whichever style is yours, it is important to remember that choosing to be childfree, just like choosing to have children, is a huge decision. It affects your entire life. Whether you lean more towards the 'analysis' or the 'lightning bolt' style of decision making, you must still really think about what the choice will mean to your life, and whether you are making the right decision.

This is not to suggest that becoming childfree is a one-time choice. I use the phrase 'becoming childfree' intentionally; in most cases, the decision almost has to be made over and over again. Even those who experience the 'lightning bolt' need to think it through occasionally, to make sure that it genuinely is the right thing for them.

A great way to decide whether being childfree is truly for you is to try it out. This is an extended version of the imagination exercise that I provided earlier in the book, and it really does work for many people. Helen describes how she and her husband tried out being childfree. "We started saying only amongst ourselves that it was nice not to have kids because we got to do various things, pointing out all the advantages to each other." As this continued, Helen says that they "started warming up to the whole idea of being a family of two." Helen and her husband had long believed that families were only families because they had children. By imagining becoming childfree, and noticing the things that would be good, they began to change this belief.

Trying on the childfree lifestyle, if it's going to work for you, needs to be done as though you have genuinely made the decision not to have children. I would suggest spending at least a month on this project. This may seem like a very long time; when you consider that you're making a decision that will affect your entire life, it's certainly a worthwhile investment.

No infertility treatments for that month. No worries about whether you're pregnant or not. In fact, if you think there is any chance that you might conceive you should use some form of contraception. I know it may seem like a waste of time and effort, but if you're truly going to try out the childfree life, you need to make it as realistic as you can. If you do become childfree, you will not *want* to have a child, and will in fact want to prevent pregnancy, so you need to test that attitude out as well.

Give this exercise as much of your attention and effort as you've given to the pursuit of pregnancy. Do all of the things that you and your partner enjoy. Go out for a nice dinner, go to a movie or play, sit and read for hours, make love whenever the mood takes you, pick up a discarded hobby or start a new one; do whatever you really want to do.

At the same time, consider whether the rest of your life is where you want it to be. Are you happy with your job? Do you like where you live? What your home is like? Have you put your life on hold while going through infertility treatments? Make a few simple and easy changes, and see how you feel.

Some people find that they immediately know that they are now on the right path, that they are no longer willing to go through infertility. For you, I strongly encourage caution and a slow pace. Please, do not make any permanent changes right away! You have spent a long time trying to have a child, and that time and effort should not be discounted. It may well be the right time for you to stop trying and to become childfree; it may also be, though, that you are just in serious need of a break. Enjoy living childfree for a time, and see whether it is truly what you want for the rest of your life.

Other people might find this break time to be incredibly difficult and stressful. It might feel like giving up, like you have nothing else to do if you're not trying for a baby, and, most painful of all, it might feel as though this would be the month that you *would* successfully conceive. Please try not to let this feeling overtake you.

The whole point of this exercise, and indeed of this entire book, is giving you back control over your life. If you feel that the right thing to do is to go back to trying to have a child, then make that happen. Try to go back with a more relaxed attitude if possible, *not* because it will necessarily make it happen faster, but because it's far better for your own mental state.

If you find yourself feeling as though you must go back to trying for a baby right away, feeling panicky and desperate, please try to take even a few more days. When I feel frantic like that, it is often a sign that I am trying to avoid examining the situation more closely. While it might not be for you, it is still important to find out why you are having those feelings.

A few days, or a month, or even six months of time away from trying to have a child will almost for sure not prevent you from having one. It is important that you allow yourself the time to think through the situation, and to genuinely feel what you're feeling.

Many emotions might arise during this process. You might feel angry that you have spent so much time on your infertility, as Katherine described above. You might feel sad at the wasted time and energy, or maybe about the damage that infertility has done to your relationships, finances, and mental state. You might feel relief at the idea of ending the infertility roller coaster. You might feel guilty about the idea of stopping.

Whatever you feel is right and normal and necessary to help you get through this situation. It *is* an unfair situation, it *is* hard and painful, and it *is* very different from what you had planned for yourself. All of these things are true. What is also true is that you have the ability to decide how you will handle the situation, and what you will do with the rest of your life. Do not give up that ability and control; they are vital!

There is a danger in spending so much time thinking about the situation, however. When I worked in information technology, we referred to it as 'analysis paralysis'. You do not want to spend your entire life thinking about this decision! My father always says, "Make your decision, and then make it the right one." Certainly, take the time you need to make the decision that's right for you, but then move on with your life in its new path.

Life as a childfree person can be absolutely wonderful; your life does not have to be less than it would have been as a parent. Different, of course, but not less. Do not settle for less! Make your life the best that it can be.

6

What Will The Childfree Life Be Like?

There is no one way to be childfree. Some people are negative towards children and parents, and become annoyed whenever they see them. Some find themselves indifferent to children; able to spend time with them when they are around but not interested in actively seeking them out. Some people enjoy being around children, or perhaps only like children of certain ages, but do not feel the need to have their own. And some have the occasional twinge of wishing that they did have children but are generally happy with their childfree lives. (Beyond this would be someone who still truly wants to have children; this person is childless, not childfree.)

Wherever you find yourself on this continuum, you can most certainly still be childfree. You may find that your childfree attitudes and beliefs change as you begin and continue your childfree life.

When I first began to explore becoming childfree, I was very negative towards children. I became frustrated and annoyed whenever I saw them, and especially whenever they seemed to be excessively noisy. As I became more comfortable with my decision, though, and worked through my lingering feelings of frustration and failure at my infertility, I began to see more of the positive things about being around children.

While I never permanently returned to the childless state, I did (and still do) experience occasional surges of sadness at not having had children. I suspect that these come with the territory for the vast majority of the childfree after infertility. While our lives are now strong and happy, we did not gain something that we had hoped for, and that can hurt.

I have found that the best way through these feelings is to sit down and really think about whether I want a child. I think through, just as I recommended in past chapters, exactly how things would change if we returned to infertility treatments, and I consider whether I want those changes to take place.

Invariably, I find very quickly that I do not truly want to have a child; instead, I am feeling jealous of someone else for the attention that they receive for their child, or I feel overwhelmed at work, or I feel bored. None of these, of course, are good reasons to have a child. Once I recognize what I am really thinking or feeling, I remind myself that I *chose* to live childfree, and think about all the wonderful things that go along with it. Very quickly, I feel better.

For many of us, the childfree life seems different and strange. We have planned to have children, and may have been expecting all of our lives that we would be parents. Infertility has changed the expected path of our lives, and it is natural to wonder what will come next.

What comes next depends in large part on what you put into it, and on what you expect your life to be like. If you see a life without children as sad, a failure, and worthless, then that is what you will have.

If, on the other hand, you take the opportunity that you have been given, things can be very different. Many people never truly decide that they want to have children. Instead, they fall into parenthood because "everyone has children", never truly deciding whether it is really right for them. You are now in the enviable position of being able to choose a new path for your life. I found this both exhilarating and terrifying all at the same time. There just seemed to be so many *options* open to me, and I wanted to do everything. Take the time to examine the options and decide how you want to recreate your life.

It seems to me that having children puts your life on a clear path, marked with milestones as your child develops. The first day of school, the first day of high school, high school graduation, attending university or college, graduation, marriage, maybe the birth of the first grandchild—while not every parent will experience each and every one of these milestones, they are points to look forward to, and a guiding structure for the parent's life. I find that my life instead feels like a huge open expanse of time, and it can be very frightening to imagine how to fill it. I want to know that my life has ben worthwhile, and while I definitely do not think that the only way, or even the best way, to make a contribution to the world is to have a child, I am now in the position of needing to decide what *I* want to do with my life to make it meaningful. Not having children does leave you with many more options than those available to a conscientious parent. You can change careers much more easily, without needing to be concerned with how your salary or work hours will affect your child. You might find yourself more willing to take on additional responsibilities at work, or choose instead to find a fulfilling hobby or activity that enriches your life. Making these choices can be uncomfortable, but it gives you the opportunity to create the life you truly want. There are many books available on how to do this, some of which are listed in Appendix A.

It can, admittedly, be difficult to visualize and create a happy childfree lifestyle for yourself if you do not know anyone who has experienced it. Ellen had a role model for the childfree lifestyle as she was growing up, and she feels that it helped her adjust. "My mother's brother and his wife were infertile and opted to live child-free. As we were a close-knit family when I was a child, I got to know a happy, well-adjusted childless couple. I saw the benefits they enjoyed from their lifestyle and how they took joy from their interactions with their nieces and nephews. I resolved to do the same."

If you do not have a role model like Ellen's, consider seeking one out. Organizations such as No Kidding!, a social group for childfree adults, have chapters all over the world, and their meetings allow you to meet other people who do not have children. While not all of these people will be childfree after infertility, some certainly are likely to be, and it can be very enjoyable to be with a group of adults without having the conversation constantly turning to children. Check Appendix A for more information on resources for the childfree, including my web site.

◆   ◆   ◆

Infertility treatments can take away a great deal of your physical energy. After infertility, the negative physical effects of infertility drugs will be gone, and so will the draining cycles of highs and lows each month as you desperately hope to become pregnant. As a childfree person, you can choose to put this reclaimed energy into other areas of your life.

Many people take up hobbies or activities that they did not previously take part in, or expand their participation in pre-existing ones. Not long after choosing to become childfree, I began belly dancing. Ironically, an art form with strong links to fertility and birth has made me feel stronger, more powerful, and more *myself* than anything else for a long time. Not having children has given me the time to pursue my dancing without feeling guilty about taking time away from them.

Other couples find that they begin exercising together, or take up a new hobby together. Infertility treatments can leave you feeling as though your body is the enemy; beginning a new physical activity, and seeing just how well you can do, helps to bring you back into your own body.

Most couples find that their sex lives are infinitely better. Freed from the timing restrictions of trying to conceive, sex can become spontaneous and joyful again. The freedom of not obsessing over whether *this time* you will get pregnant makes everything better. And, of course, there is no worrying about being interrupted by the children!

Financially, your life may be far easier as well. Estimates on what it costs to raise a child to adulthood vary wildly, but no matter how you measure it, it is incredibly expensive. Choosing not to have children means that you can either apply those resources elsewhere in your life or you can choose to not *earn* as much. For example, I left my job in information technology to become a teacher, taking a substantial pay cut but greatly increasing my job satisfaction.

◆   ◆   ◆

Maureen told me, "My husband had a vasectomy and we are definitely 'childfree'. I won't say that I never have twinges about 'what would it have been like', but I don't consider my life a failure because I don't have kids either." My experiences mirror Maureen's, and those of many other people. I have stressed that becoming childfree is a *process*, not a destination, and this is very important to keep in mind. Please do not expect that you will never again feel a longing for a child, never again wish that things had worked out differently, never again feel childless.

Unfortunately, you will feel all of these things from time to time. Sometimes, when I'm teaching, I find myself wishing that a particular student could have been mine, that I could experience the joys of parenting and feel the full pride in that student that a parent would. At other times, when my students are being difficult, I am very glad that I do not have full responsibility for these children at all times.

These twinges, though, are rare. People who have truly chosen to be childfree do not find themselves endlessly obsessing with 'what could have been'. They are moving ahead with their lives. Thinking back to Joyce's lemonade analogy in Chapter 3, they are not sad about not being able to add a bit more sugar to their lemonade. Instead, they are enjoying the lemonade that they already have, and finding new and interesting things to add to the mix.

I know for myself that infertility prevented me from a life that would truly not have been as good for my husband and me, and I am honestly glad that I went through it. It gave me a chance to live my life on my own terms, and to genuinely choose what I wanted to do and who I wanted to be. This can be very difficult, but it has also been very rewarding. I feel blessed.

I know it can be hard to imagine infertility as a blessing. Nonetheless, I have spoken to many people who do feel lucky that they were thwarted in their attempts to have a child. Helen, for example, told me, "I wouldn't like to go through the infertility wringer again but it has made me who I am today. I came out on the other side a better person for it." Others told me of how much stronger their marriages became as a result of working through infertility together.

Unfortunately, this is not always the case. Cathy, for example, told me that she did not feel supported by her husband during infertility. She said, "I know my husband isn't completely in agreement with me, but he did little in this battle, while I fought to the very edge at times." While it is generally true that women *do* have to take a more active role in infertility treatment, it also does seem to be the case that husbands are usually far more passive in terms of pursuing treatment.

This may be because husbands are often not as committed to having a child. There are, of course, exceptions to this; Alice told me that *she* was not driven to have a child and only went through infertility treatments because her husband truly wanted children. Nonetheless, the majority of the women who spoke to me told me that they did not think that their husbands were as interested in having a child. This was certainly the case for me. While Wes was supportive and caring, and did what I asked in terms of doctor visits and testing, he was doing these things *for me*, not because he truly wanted a child. Even at the time, he did let me know that he would be happy if we had a child and just as happy if we did not.

This did not sit well with me at all, because there was nothing more important to me than having a child. I could not understand how he could be so casual about something that, no matter how it turned out, would have such a huge impact on our lives. I wanted him to care as much as I did, to be as devastated when I did not become pregnant, to really feel what I was feeling. (Interestingly, when I showed Wes this part of the book, he said, "I wasn't casual! I was just more open to the other possibilities than you were." I truly did believe that he *was* unconcerned and casual, and I think this shows that you do need to keep your lines of communication open and honest during infertility and into the childfree life.)

Once you have moved past infertility and into becoming childfree, however, you may find that your relationship becomes much happier and stronger than it has ever been. Having survived, together, something as difficult as infertility can really bring a couple together. Once it became obvious that I was no longer able to continue trying to have a child, Wes and I were able to openly discuss our feelings and the childfree alternative. It has strengthened our relationship immensely, and we are able to work through the other twists and turns in our lives in a similar fashion. Going through infertility taught us to be open and honest with each other.

Unfortunately, infertility can also tear you apart, if you and your partner are not in agreement about becoming childfree. If this happens to you, it is vital that you talk openly and honestly. Counselling might be necessary as well, *not* to convince one of you to change, but to get at the roots of what you are both feeling and to find a way to work things out. Do not try to persuade your partner to go against what he or she truly wants, but do work together to find out whether there is a way to make both of you happy.

It does need to be said, regrettably, that some marriages do not survive infertility. Rose and her husband separated soon after her repeated miscarriages. He suggested adoption, which she was not comfortable investigating, but was very busy with his career and not really available to her emotionally. While he said that he wanted children, she was the one investigating all of the possible treatments and making the decisions, while he essentially did only what she asked him to do. While there are naturally two sides to every story, Rose definitely felt abandoned and alone, and these feelings most certainly contributed to the end of her marriage. Again, I suggest that, if infertility and its aftermath are putting unbearable strain on your relationship, you find some form of counselling or therapy that can help you to work through it together. (Do be cautious, though—I have heard of situations in which the therapist basically said, "You're being selfish, just have a child." *This* sort of 'help' is unprofessional and worse than useless.)

◆   ◆   ◆

I found that my biggest emotional issue during the early stages of becoming childfree was a strong sense that I had 'given up'. My husband and I chose not to go into any stronger fertility drugs than Clomid, or into IUI, IVF, or any other in-depth procedures. I have never been one to give up on a challenge, and I really did feel that I was throwing in the towel too easily on this one.

What I eventually realized, and what I hope you will realize *earlier* than I did, is that everyone has their own limit, their own point where they truly cannot do any more. I know a woman who spent ten years going through infertility, and every treatment imaginable, before finally choosing to live (very happily) childfree. Had I done that, I would honestly have lost both my marriage and my sanity. I spent nearly a year dealing with infertility and that was more than enough.

Choosing to stop treatment is *not* quitting, and it is *not* giving up. It is making a decision, based on the information that you have, that you think will be the best one for you, and then moving forward.

I obsessed for a while over the thought that the next cycle would have been the one where I would have had a baby. I think many people do this when they stop trying to have a child. However, the fact is that the other cycles did not work, and this one, in and of itself, is no different than the others. It just happens to be the one where you decided that you had had enough.

Please do not feel that you gave in too soon, or that you weren't tough enough to stick it out. No matter how long you dealt with infertility, you have been through it, and have come out the other side ready not just to survive, but to thrive. Be proud of yourself for making it through, and don't judge how much you 'took' compared to what other people did.

WHAT WILL HAPPEN WHEN YOU GROW OLD?

Many newly childfree people are very concerned about who will take care of them when they are elderly. As a society, we tend to believe that children are always there to take care of their parents as they age, and that those of us who do not have children will be at risk of being completely alone.

This possibility naturally concerned me as well, so I looked into various studies assessing how well the childfree (or 'childless', as nearly every study terms them) do as they age. The result? We need not worry. (The references for all of the studies cited below are included in Appendix C.)

Mueller and Yoder (1999) reported that childless people were seen as selfish, abnormal, moody, bitter, less loving, leading unfulfilling lives, and were perceived to be miserable in their old age. However, not one of these perceptions has been found to be accurate when studies have been done. In fact, one study actually found that having children *reduced* happiness. Mueller and Yoder also found that the childfree tend to do better than mothers on tests of marital happiness, and that they more often say that they feel happy and positive.

Zhang and Hayward (2001) report on many studies which showed that the childfree do not have significantly different levels of life satisfaction than parents, and that the childfree are also not significantly more lonely and depressed. However, they did note that there is a difference depending on whether 'childlessness' is voluntary or involuntary. While our infertility was involuntary, we are now choosing to live a new life, and are choosing to be childfree. A true choice in this direction does make your 'childlessness' voluntary, as you are now choosing to remain without a child.

When you do this, you will naturally find that you seek out other people who do not have children, as we all like to have friends who are similar to us. When this happens, you begin to create a social support network of people on whom you can rely. Parents usually expect their children to be a large part of their support network; we create our own in our choices of friends and acquaintances. As well, we realize that we will not have children to support us in our old age, and do not expect that to happen. Many parents who *do* expect it may find themselves shocked and hurt by their children's indifference. As Katherine told me,

> "People ask if I worry about who will take care of me when I am no longer able to take care of myself. I tell them that nursing homes are filled with people with children, people who wait day after day for their children to visit.
>
> A close friend of mine is a nursing home administrator who delivered some shocking news to me one day. She said that she couldn't count the times that she is told by residents' children not to be notified unless their parent(s) are dead.
>
> She said more often than not, it is the friends who sign people into the facility and it is the friends who visit most often."

It is horrible that many children are not supporting their parents as they age. It does, however, mean that we will not necessarily be the only ones without children by our sides.

Connidis and McMullin (1993) also found that it was important whether or not you felt that you had chosen not to have children. If you did not feel that the decision had been within your control, you were more likely to be depressed as an elderly person than if you *did* feel that you had made the choice yourself.

These researchers also found that the people they referred to as 'childless by circumstance' were less happy than parents, regardless of whether the parents felt that they had good relationships with their children. Parents who do *not* think that they have good relationships with their offspring are less happy than those who do, and the childfree are not significantly different in terms of their happiness than those who are close to their children.

◆   ◆   ◆

So, what does all of this mean to us? I think it means that everyone creates, to a large extent, their own lives, and that we each have an opportunity, and a responsibility, to find supports for ourselves. In some cases, those supports are children, but in many others, they are other family members and friends. My mother-in-law, for example, spent a great deal of time and effort helping a great-aunt and great-uncle who had no children. She took care of them, made sure that they were eating properly, and in general helped them to live out their lives in dignity and with their pride intact.

Please bear in mind, as well, that you *might* end up regretting not having children, just as many parents do end up regretting *having* them. I would far rather regret not having had them, given the choice between the two.

Finally, consider Wendy's experience. She told me, "In retrospect, I think I may have just wanted to fulfill society's (and my parents') expectations of me. I am now 52, about to retire from public school teaching/counseling, still married to the same man after 27.5 years, and completely contented to be childfree."

7

"Why Don't You Just Adopt?":
Dealing With Others

I have often thought that it would be far easier to deal with becoming childfree after infertility if I never had to leave my home or speak to another person other than my husband. I am confident that we have made the right decision in choosing not to have children; somehow, though, that certainty seems to desert me at times when I am discussing my choices with others.

All people who choose not to have children face some degree of questioning or criticism from others. It is not surprising, since most people *do* have children. People who do not may seem strange or even threatening to parents.

For those of us who come to the childfree lifestyle after infertility, however, the situation can be even more extreme. People who know that we did want children, or know that we were trying to conceive, may be confused about our new decision to remain childfree. Even people who do not know about our infertility might still think that we would be good parents, and be surprised that we are not choosing that route.

As we have already seen, becoming childfree after infertility is not an easy process, and it requires a great deal of thought and soul-searching. It is important not to forget what you have learned about yourself as you move into your childfree lifestyle. You are almost certain to face at least some questioning, and remaining sure of yourself and your reasons for your decision can be difficult. As Cathy told me, "I know many of my friends and family still don't understand why I've 'given up', and they still make some comments." Depending on your personality and the person asking the questions, there are many possible responses. We will discuss some of them below.

First, though, I want to touch on the most common one, and the most difficult to answer—"Isn't it selfish not to have children?" It can be very hard to respond to this question because many responses end up making you feel as though you're being defensive. Here's how I respond to this question, which I have been asked on several occasions.

I take a deep breath so that I can stay calm and rational during the discussion, and then I say, in as neutral a tone as I can manage, "Selfish to whom?" My questioner is usually taken aback, and might eventually say "to your husband" or "to your parents". My response to *that* is that it is 'selfish' to try to make someone else do something that they do not want to do just because *you* want that thing to have been done. It is not selfish for me to make a choice that is good for me and does not hurt someone else. I often follow up with, "I think it is far more selfish to *have* a child and then not give them the proper care, love, and attention that they deserve, as so many people do, than it is to choose not to have them." Feel free to borrow this response!

STRANGERS AND ACQUAINTANCES

Dealing with the comments of those we don't know well is usually easier than handling family and friends. Acquaintances generally do not take your decision to remain childfree personally, and are usually able to separate your decision from their own lifestyle choices.

Did you notice the many qualifiers in the previous paragraph? Ironically, acquaintances can also be the ones who make the most painful and difficult to handle comments. Since they don't know us well, they may not be aware of our infertility. This may result in comments that are unintentionally cutting and distressing.

During my infertility, for example, two of my colleagues became pregnant accidentally. Listening to them bemoan their fate was nearly unbearable for me. I had made a conscious decision to keep my situation to myself at work, so I knew that these women were not aware of what was happening in my life. Nonetheless, it was so hard to hear them complaining about something that I was doing everything I could to achieve.

I also often find that people will ask me, "How many children do you have?" rather than "Do you have children?" Since many women do have children, I understand why the question is presented in this way. It is still hard to hear and respond to, though, especially during the thick of infertility.

I used to launch into a detailed explanation of how I wanted a child but wasn't able to have one, and hoped I'd be able to someday. Once I decided for sure to remain childfree, I changed the explanation to describe that I had wanted a child but hadn't been able to have one, and was now happy without one. The length and excessive detail of the explanation, unfortunately, remained the same. Now, I simply smile sweetly and cheerfully say, "None, just cats!" I find people usually start talking about their own pets, and the 'child issue' is defused. Some people even say, "Wow, good for you! Kids are so much work!"

While this 'distraction' approach is usually successful, there are times when it doesn't work. I had a doctor tell me that there was obviously something wrong with my marriage since I no longer wanted to go through infertility. It was all I could do to refrain from telling him that stopping treatments was the first good thing to happen to my marriage in a long time!

In this sort of situation, I think it is important to stay calm and rational. Allowing the person to upset you (especially when the person is a stranger) is not going to improve the situation in any way. When I hear insensitive comments from others, I try to figure out where the person is coming from and why they feel the need to make such comments. I keep my answers simple and unemotional, and I walk away from the person as soon as I can. (I told the doctor, "My marriage is fine, and I no longer want to go through treatments." He looked doubtful, but did stop asking me questions.) Other suggestions include: asking in a cool voice, "Why do you want to know?", changing the topic, and first saying, "My, that's a personal question!" and then changing the topic.

Some of the other responses that I have heard of people using are more assertive, or even aggressive, but they do seem to get results. I would say that you should consider the source of the comment and the likely motivation for it before choosing to use one of these responses.

I quite like, "We would have children, but the cat is allergic". I think it is similar in tone to my "None, just cats!" response, without being overly aggressive. I have also tried "You know Wes and I, do you *really* think the world needs a combination of us?" with good success, and I have heard of people saying, "I cannot bear children" in a completely neutral tone, leaving the questioner to guess whether you mean that you cannot get pregnant or that you cannot stand children. This response does seem to work for some people.

What I do *not* suggest is telling people that you are unable to get pregnant. While it might seem that this statement would stop the discussion, I have heard far too often that it actually leads to an endless stream of unwanted advice. "Why don't you try this treatment? That doctor? This position? This herbal remedy? That therapist?"

I used to be ashamed that I could not get pregnant. I am not ashamed any more, and so I do feel comfortable telling people, briefly, when the situation warrants it, "I did try to have children, but it was going to be very difficult for me, so we thought about it and decided we were happier the way we were." I say this calmly and with conviction, and I have rarely had anyone someone challenge me on it.

FRIENDS

Unfortunately, it can be far more difficult if the person asking the questions is a close friend. These are people who usually want the best for us and want us to be happy. They may be aware of all that you have been through, and may not understand why you are 'giving up' on your dream.

If you sit down with a good friend and really discuss what is happening in your life, and why you really do need to stop trying to have a baby, the chances are good that a real friend will understand and support you. I have run into difficulties in the past when I *expected* my friends to understand my situation without my taking the time to explain it to them and to really let them in on what I was feeling. Even really good friends are not mind readers, after all, and they cannot really be expected to support us when they do not completely understand the situation.

It is from friends, though, that I have received the response, "Oh, you'll change your mind". What an infuriating thing to say! It is always on the tip of my tongue to say, "Why, are you going to change your mind about having had your children?", but I have never said it, despite feeling *very* tempted.

I think that this response comes from people finding it difficult to imagine that anyone doesn't have children. New parents and people who plan to have children very soon are far more likely to be sure that you will change your mind, but this response really can come from anyone who sees having children as a necessary part of life.

It can be very difficult for the formerly infertile to respond to, as we *did* want children, and frankly *might* still change our minds and decide that we want to resume infertility treatment. I suggest that you do not respond with a fervent denial, as it might come back to haunt you later. At this stage in my own child-free journey, I *would* respond with a definite, "No, I won't, because I'm very happy with my life now." If you feel that you can honestly make this response, wonderful! I used to say, "Well, I don't think that I will, but if I do, I'll work something out." This response seemed to let the questioner know that I had considered the possibility of changing my mind and was ready to deal with it should it occur.

A good friend is most likely just trying to look out for your welfare with this question. Still, it does feel insulting, because it implies that you haven't really given this decision any thought. If the questioning continued, I would make that clear, and tell the person, "I have given this decision a great deal of time and effort, more than most people put into choosing to have a child, and I am confident that I have made the right decision. If it does turn out later that I want to change the decision, I will, and I will do whatever needs to be done. For now, though, I see no chance that I will change my mind. Thank you for being worried about me, but I'm fine." This sort of assertive response will most likely end the conversation. If it does not, the person has other motives than simply concern for you.

I once had quite a long discussion with a coworker, in which she remained certain that I *would* change my mind, and nothing that I could say seemed to dissuade her from this belief. I learned a few months later that she had been in the midst of deciding whether or not she wanted to have a child, and that she was now pregnant. Perhaps she was trying to convince herself to have a child more than trying to convince me?

I also had one interesting situation where a friend simply didn't *hear* me say that I would not be having children. She asked when I planned to have them, and I said, "We aren't going to." "Oh, not for a few years, right? That makes sense," she answered. I didn't know what to say for a minute, and then I said, "No, we aren't going to have them at all." "Not *ever*?" she replied. No, not ever. She seemed a bit surprised, but did accept my response.

It must be said, however, that you *might* lose some friendships as a result of your decision to remain childfree. Some people cannot understand and accept that you have chosen a different path from theirs, and they might pressure you to change your mind. They might see your decision as a rejection of the path they have chosen, and be angry that you seem to be turning away from them.

If a friend is not enjoying being a parent, they might envy you, and feel guilty about that envy and about not being as happy to have a child as they had expected. In this case, they might pressure you even more, because if you did have children they would have someone to commiserate with.

You might also, especially in the early days of your decision, find it painful to be around children. Many childfree people have told me that all of their friends seemed to be having children right around the time that they were dealing with infertility. At this time, and even as you begin to move into the childfree lifestyle, it can be very difficult to be near children. It is especially painful, as several people told me, if you and a friend began trying to have a baby at the same time, and the friend conceived quickly. Every time you see that child, you imagine what your own child would have been like at that age. This, naturally, can make it very difficult to be around that particular friend.

This is not to say that it is impossible for a childfree person to be friends with parents. My friend Angela, whose baby I described in Chapter 1, is still a very good friend of mine even now that she is a mother. When I found out that she was going to have a baby, I was very concerned, because I had already lost two friends due to parenthood and couldn't stand the thought of losing Angela as well. But that didn't happen. How did we manage to stay friends?

By the time Angela had her baby, I had been committed for nearly three years to being childfree. I had worked through a lot of my pain and frustration about not being able to conceive, and was well on the way to building a really happy and enjoyable life for myself. I found myself able to share Angela's happiness about her pregnancy without being too overwhelmed with my previous jealousy of all pregnant women.

As well, I think both Angela and I try hard to make it work. One of the other friends that I lost due to parenthood spent a great deal of time telling me how wonderful it was to have a baby, and how *sad* it was that I hadn't been able to do it, and how *badly* she felt for me that I wouldn't be able to have all of the joys that she was experiencing. When I finally managed to say something about being childfree now, she responded with, "Oh, I think it's so funny when people put a label on themselves to make themselves feel better." That was the last time I saw this particular person.

Angela has never once made me feel as though she is now better than I am because she has a child. She is the same person that she's always been, and now she has Maggie too. When we are together, we do talk about Maggie a lot, but we also talk about our marriages, our houses, our jobs, our *lives*. Angela is a mother now, and that is a big part of her life, but it is not her whole life, and I respect that.

Angela also clearly respects my choices. As a result, I feel comfortable sitting and playing with Maggie or reading her stories, because I know that Angela is not secretly thinking, "Oh, how sweet! It's really too bad Heather didn't ever have a baby." I respect her and her husband for having really thought out their decision to have a child, and they respect Wes and I for the same reason.

I do also have to admit that I have been more flexible in my friendship with Angela than I have been in the past. While Angela is very organized, and keeps

'Maggie disruptions' to a minimum, it is naturally more difficult for two women and a two-year-old to go out than for two women alone. As well, our visits nearly always take place at Angela's house, because it's easier than bringing Maggie to my (non-child-proofed!) home.

So, I do certainly believe that it is possible for a childfree person and a parent to be friends, and good friends, but it does take flexibility and respect on both sides. In the very early days of your becoming childfree, it might be too much to handle, however. Be good to yourself, and do not force yourself to spend time with children if it is extremely painful to you.

FAMILY

It can be very difficult to know what to tell family members, particularly parents and in-laws, about your infertility. On the one hand, they love you, and generally do want what is best for you. On the other hand, they naturally have expectations about how you will live your life, and your choosing not to have children may not go along with what they expect.

Many parents have long dreamed of the day when they would become grandparents. Your decision not to have children has taken that day away from them. If you are an only child, or if none of your siblings are in a position to have children, this can be even more difficult for your parents to accept. While it *is* your decision, they may feel compelled to help you 'see the error of your ways'.

Amber had this experience. When she told her parents that she and her husband Colin would not be having children, and that she would be having a tubal ligation to make sure that she would never have them, her parents were initially very calm and understanding, and Amber felt relieved and happy that they were so supportive.

The next day, however, things changed. Amber's parents called her and tried to convince her to change her mind. Amber recalls, "They said, 'What if something happens to Colin? What will you do then? Why doesn't *he* have the surgery instead of you?' I felt very angry, and I really felt betrayed." Amber's parents eventually did accept the situation, but it has never been discussed again.

Amber's story brings up a very important question. How much should you tell your family about your infertility and your resolution to it? If Amber and Colin had not told Amber's parents before the surgery, they would not have been pressured in the same way. However, Amber's parents might have been even more upset if they had not been told until *after* the surgery was complete.

It is a very difficult question, and the right answer really depends on you and your relationships with your family members. If your parents have always been very supportive of you and your decisions, then they might also be supportive here. If they have always seemed to believe that they knew best, they might not be ready or able to support you.

In the end, it really is your decision. My husband and I did tell both sets of parents before the surgery, because we felt that making the announcement would be both a definite statement that we were serious and an opportunity to bring the situation out into the open and make sure that our families understood that we had carefully considered all possibilities. My parents were concerned that we might not completely understand that this was permanent, and worried that we might change our minds. Being able to discuss with them how we had come to the decision did help to allay their fears.

On the other hand, Helen told me, "We did not tell anyone about Malcolm's vasectomy, and we do not plan on it. We figure that it is none of their business anyway. Our families think we'll change our minds or that some miracle will occur. Have I got news for them!"

Regardless of whether or not you choose to tell your family about your infertility and its resolution, they will most likely question you about your lack of children. Some parents will see your decision as a criticism of how they raised you, or a rejection of their own values, even more than your friends may have done.

It is important to realize that, just as you needed time to grieve the loss of your dream of a child, your parents and family need that time as well. If they knew about your infertility, they have most likely been cheering you on and being hopeful right along with you throughout it all, and the end of your efforts for a child means the end of a dream for them. At the same time, they do need to realize that you are the only one who truly has the right to choose whether to continue treatment, and that you need to do what is right for you.

Unfortunately, sometimes your family may not be supportive at all. They might insist that you will change your mind, tell you that you will regret your decision, make you feel guilty for not providing them with grandchildren, or simply act as though you have ruined their lives. I have even heard of parents offering five thousand dollars if the couple changed their minds and decided to have a child!

There is really very little that you can do if this sort of thing happens, sadly. I cannot tell you whether to cut ties with your family, or whether it would be worthwhile trying to make them understand your point of view. It naturally depends on the way your relationship has been to this point.

Remember, though, that it *is* your decision whether or not to have children, and you need to hold onto that. You would be the ones raising the children, responsible for them for the rest of your lives, not your family. No matter how they feel about it, it has to be your decision in the end. Take the time to make the right decision for you, and then make it clear to your family that this is how it will be.

As Karla told me, "I have decided to take a break from it all and live my life for me for awhile. This was a very hard decision to come to as friends and family do not seem to understand my wanting to stop until I have exhausted every possibility. But, I can't do it anymore. It wasn't good for my emotional or physical well being and it was definitely putting some pressure on our marriage." You know what you can handle, and what you are willing to accept, and that is how it needs to be.

◆   ◆   ◆

I personally feel that one of the rudest and most unfeeling comments that can be made to someone who is childfree after infertility is the dreaded, "Why don't you just adopt?", because it is disrespectful on so many levels. It implies that you didn't even consider adoption, and that adoption is a quick and easy solution to infertility. I am lucky in that I have never been asked this question, but I would reply with something to the effect of, "If your husband died tomorrow, would you just go out and pick up a new one?"

I did not seriously investigate adoption as a resolution to my infertility, because I knew, *for me*, that a big part of my desire to have children was to see myself and my family in my child. I wanted to spend time gazing at my child, trying to decide whether she had my father's eyes or my mother's chin, and whether she looked more like me or like my husband when we were babies. I would not have been able to have any of this had I adopted.

While I was going through infertility, however, a coworker was going through an international adoption. I had a vague idea that it was 'difficult' to adopt. I had no idea at all just how incredibly time-consuming, expensive, invasive, and nerve-wracking it really is. This woman and her husband were interviewed repeatedly by various social workers and counsellors, they had their home inspected to make sure it would be fit for a child, they had to pay a great deal of money, and the entire process took well over a year. I am so pleased for them that it did work out, and that they have a lovely little daughter, but it is an incredibly demanding process that should not be undertaken lightly.

Katherine told me, "People ask why we don't adopt. Adoption was not the right choice for us. Neither my husband nor I could imagine raising another couple's child. We wanted a child that we would have created together, beginning from one cell created from a bond of perfect love and perfect trust. An adopted child is a human being, with thoughts, feelings, and emotions. Wouldn't it be terrible if that child felt that they were 'second best?' No, we could not do that to another human being."

By no means am I implying that adoption is not a perfectly valid choice. It most certainly is. But it is a choice that should only be entered into by those who understand what it will be like and are ready for it, and not every infertile person fits the bill.

◆   ◆   ◆

I strongly suggest that you do spend at least a little time considering possible responses to the various questions that you might be asked. While you certainly do not need to have a speech memorized, having some idea of what you might say will make you a little more comfortable when the questions are asked, and you will be more able to make a response that does get your point across without being rude.

Consider your own personality carefully and make your response fit. I was interviewed by a radio station, along with two other childfree adults, both of whom were quite vocal about their negative feelings about children. When the program was aired, the announcer began by saying, "Some people really dislike children. Some people tell everyone. And some people do it with humour, by having a bumper sticker that reads, 'If I wanted to hear the pitter patter of little feet, I'd put shoes on the cat!'". That is my bumper sticker.

At first, I felt silly and embarrassed, but then I realized that the announcer had made a very good point. That *is* my style. The more assertive or even aggressive responses do not work for me, an elementary school teacher who genuinely does like my students, but the humourous ones do. My "none, just cats" response, just like my bumper sticker, gets the point across without being unkind or rude, and that works for me. Decide what works for you, and be prepared, because you *will* be faced with at least some questions!

8

The Journey Continues

At this point, we have been through what infertility does to your life, how you can go about choosing to move from infertility into a joyous life, and what that new life can be like. I want to leave you with some reminders of what you have read in the previous chapters, and with my sincere hopes that you will be able to move on from your infertility and create a truly happy life for yourself.

If you have not already done so, please do take the time to work carefully through the questions in Chapter 2. If you really think about each question, and answer them honestly, they can reveal a lot about how you are currently thinking and feeling about having a child. Do not be surprised if your answers to these questions change as you move into becoming childfree—they reflect your true feelings about having a child. Also, Appendix A lists a number of other resources that might be helpful to you in assessing whether you truly do want to continue with infertility treatments.

When you begin to see yourself as *childfree* rather than *childless*, your life will begin to change. Becoming childfree opens up a wide range of possibilities about how you will live your life, and this can be frightening. Try instead to see it as an opportunity to create a life that really matters to you, and take the time to find what you truly want to do with your life. Be open as well to the possibility that there may be *several* things that you will choose to do. I am considering retiring within the next few years (certainly by age forty) to work part time and volunteer rather than working full time. Having children would have made this extremely difficult if not impossible. Be open to the opportunities that arise for you!

Please also remember that you *do* have a choice in becoming childfree. Infertility may have taken away your ability to easily have children, but it is still up to you how far you take treatment, what sorts of treatments you take, and what your life becomes after infertility. You can even choose to remain childless, and sadly some people do. They stay miserable and let their lives just happen because they 'have no control'. You *do* have control, even if it is not as much control as you would have liked, and it is up to you to take charge and recreate your life.

Think through the various issues involved in becoming childfree, and do consider doing a 'childfree experiment' as described in Chapter 5 to see whether it is really for you. The longer you can spend in this experiment, living as though you are now childfree, the better, because the picture that it will give you will be more realistic. Do be careful, though, not to spend the rest of your life going back and forth on the decision. Think it through, consider all of the possibilities, and then make your choice and move ahead with your life.

If you find yourself one day *certain* that you should have had a child, carefully consider the state of the rest of your life. I find that I become 'childless' again, briefly, when faced with a huge change in my life or a situation that I find difficult to deal with. This might happen to you as well, maybe not for the same reasons, but it might happen nonetheless.

Please do not jump right back into trying to have a baby! You made the decision to become childfree for some very valid reasons, and those reasons have not gone away just because you are feeling childless. Think about what, if anything, has changed in your life to make you now want a child again, and then decide whether it is a true change or whether you, like me during times of stress, are feeling overwhelmed and afraid. This is a huge decision, and it deserves all of the time and attention that you can give it, without becoming bogged down. You do not want to spend the rest of your life saying, "I am childfree for now but I can't make any permanent changes in case I decide later to have kids." Instead, make the choice and move on, knowing that, if you *do* change your mind later, you will be able to work it out.

After much soul-searching, my husband and I decided in 2000 that we were definitely not going to have children, and he made an appointment to have a vasectomy. Up until about two weeks before the surgery, I was very confident that we were making the right decision. At that point, though, my world fell apart around me. I *knew* that we were doing the wrong thing, and that my life would be a complete and utter failure if I did not have a child.

Luckily, I retained just enough sanity to reach out for help instead of giving in right away to my desire for a child. I found the wonderful book, *The Parenthood Decision* by Beverly Engel, and worked conscientiously through its questions. Wes and I talked endlessly, trying to reason out why I had suddenly changed my mind. Did I just have cold feet, or were we really making the wrong decision?

Wes did have the surgery as scheduled. When he came out and told me it was finished, I felt such a strong sense of *peace*. I knew then, for sure, that we had made the right decision. I cannot imagine that I will ever change my mind again, but if I do, or if Wes does, we will work through it together.

What your life will be like as a childfree person is very much up to you. You will have a lot more freedom than parents have, but you will also have a lot more responsibility for creating a structure and pattern for your life. This can be scary, but can also be absolutely wonderful. You have the freedom to create and live a life that truly fits you, one that you will love. Take the opportunity!

You do need to have your reasons for becoming childfree clear in your own mind, because people are almost certainly going to question you. If you are lucky, they will be asking only because they care about you and want the best for you. If you are not so fortunate, they will be trying to convince you that you are doing the wrong thing.

Do not allow this to happen! You have spent a great deal of time and energy pursuing your dream of having a child, and are now choosing a new life. You have *not* made this decision lightly, even if you are of the 'struck by lightning' group described in Chapter 5, and your decision deserves respect. The vast majority of parents do not put as much energy into choosing to have children, and you should not accept people criticizing your decision or trying to make you feel guilty. Stand your ground, be polite but firm, and do what you need to do to keep your life on its new track.

◆   ◆   ◆

Ellen said, "Child-freedom is a lifelong journey; it doesn't simply end when the decision is made to pursue the lifestyle", and I completely agree. As I have already said, I do occasionally feel twinges of 'what might have been', but that is all they are, twinges. My life is on a new path, and it is great. As Cathy told me, "I don't feel like a failure, month after month. I can focus on my life as it is now, because it's not going to be suddenly drastically changed 'when I get pregnant'. I have a long way to go on the journey to find happiness childfree. But it's the direction I'm headed in, and I'm not looking back."

It is true that your life is not going to be exactly what you had expected. I will never be a mother, and I will never experience a great many moments and events that I had expected would be a very big part of my life. But I am well on my way to creating a different, but wonderful, life for myself, and my wish for you is that you will find your own way to make a joyous life.

APPENDIX A

Resources For The Childfree Lifestyle

BOOKS ABOUT THE CHILDFREE LIFE

The books that have been written about the childfree lifestyle are generally either books of people's stories, or discussions of how and why society 'cheats' the childfree. No other books focus specifically on the previously infertile and becoming childfree. Nonetheless, some of these books might be useful to you as you become childfree. I have not included books that are focused primarily on infertility.

My first recommendation is *The Parenthood Decision: Deciding Whether You Are Ready and Willing to Become a Parent* by Beverly Engel (Doubleday, 1998). Some reviews of this book have seen it as one-sided, focusing only on the negative aspects of parenthood. I honestly did not find it to be that way at all. I found that putting the time into carefully considering each of its questions, and looking at what my answers told me about why I wanted a child, really did help me to make a careful and reasoned decision about whether to continue infertility treatments.

I have read only one novel with an openly childfree main character: Gloria Bowman's *Human Slices* (Xlibris Corporation, 2001). I really enjoyed this novel, and have actually read it several times, finding something new and interesting each time. The main character does get into discussions about why she has chosen not to have children, and she comes up with some very good responses to the questioners! I know of one more novel, written by Wendy Tokunaga, called *No Kidding* (iUniverse.com, 2000). I have not yet read this book, but the reviews are very positive!

Terri Casey's *Pride and Joy: The Lives and Passions of Women without Children* (Beyond Words Publishing, 1998) contains interviews with twenty-five women who chose not to have children. Each woman speaks in her own words, describing how she came to the childfree lifestyle. While this is an excellent and inspiring book, none of the women is identified as being childfree after infertility. Many of the formerly infertile with whom I have spoken struggle with the concept of being able to *choose* to be childfree after infertility in the way that these women chose to be childfree. Still, the stories are interesting, and do show how wonderful the childfree lifestyle can be.

The book that has probably received the most attention recently is Elinor Burkett's *The Baby Boon: How Family-Friendly America Cheats the Childless* (The Free Press, 2000). A strongly worded statement of the benefits that parents receive simply by virtue of being parents, this book has provoked much-needed discussion. However, its strident tone and lack of understanding for the difficulties of parenting make it an uncomfortable read for the formerly infertile, and it does not provide any advice on choosing to be childfree. While an interesting read at times, I do not recommend it to anyone early in his or her childfree journey.

The Childless Revolution: What It Means to Be Childless Today by Madelyn Cain (Perseus Publishing, 2001) divides 'childless' women (many of whom are actually childfree) into three groups: by choice, by chance, or by happenstance. Her 'by chance' category includes the infertile. Unfortunately, the women whom she profiles in this category are most emphatically not childfree, as indicated by comments such as "they all agree they will never get over their loss, they will only adjust to it". I have spoken to many formerly infertile people who have very much gotten over their loss, and who in many cases actually no longer view infertility *as* a loss.

Laura Carroll's *Families of Two: Interviews with Happily Married Couples Without Children by Choice* (Xlibris Corporation, 2000) takes you through the stories of a number of couples who have chosen not to have children. While I like the concept of the book, I found it disappointing that there was no commentary on the couples and their stories; instead, the couples were all asked a set of questions, and their answers were presented as they were given. This book *does* have the advantage of being focused on couples, while *Pride and Joy* focuses solely on women, but I still feel that *Pride and Joy* is the better book.

A topic discussed even less than the childfree in general is childfree men. *The Chosen Lives of Childfree Men* by Patricia Lunneborg (Bergin & Garvey, 1999) does an excellent job of examining the reasons that men may choose not to have children, and how that choice affects their lives. While not specifically focused on infertility, the book is still a very interesting read, and does give insight into how men view the childfree lifestyle.

Finally, *Sweet Grapes: How to Stop Being Infertile and Start Living Again* by Jean W. Carter and Michael Carter (Perspectives Press, 1989). This book does provide a good explanation of how a person can move from being infertile to becoming childfree. Unfortunately, however, a large portion of the book is taken up with how to adopt. Adoption is definitely not for everyone, and is emphatically not the same thing as living childfree. As well, I have spoken to some people who found this book depressing, because they felt that the authors had become resigned to their childlessness rather than having actively chosen the childfree lifestyle. Not everyone who commented to me about this book felt this way, so it might be a good one for you.

BOOKS ABOUT LIFE CHANGES

Every bookstore has piles of books about how to change your life. The few that I am recommending here are the ones that I used in deciding to become an elementary school teacher (a career which I absolutely love), and so I know that they work, *if* you answer their questions honestly.

Barbara Sher's *I Could Do Anything If I Only Knew What It Was: How to Discover What You Really Want and How to Get It* (DTP, 1995) is an incredibly helpful book. As I wrote in my review on Amazon.com: "It is about analysing yourself, to see what you liked doing and were good at back throughout your life (and I was only 27 when I used it, so you don't have to be able to go that far 'back'!) It's an absolutely wonderful book, which saved me from a dull and unfulfilling but high-paying career. I'm now in one that I ADORE and am great at. Well worth reading!"

The book walks you through a series of exercises and questions that help you decide what you are good at and what you enjoy doing. It does *not* give you a career recommendation at the end of the process; rather, you put together your career choice based on what you learn as you go through the book.

This is why it is so important to answer the questions honestly and take your responses seriously. I went through all of the exercises and realized that I have always been a teacher in one capacity or another, and that I have always enjoyed it. Based on this, I decided that I would become a university professor. A very appropriate career, no doubt, except that I did not feel excited about it at all.

After I went through my answers again, I realized that children had also always been part of my life, and that they were not being taken into account in my new career plan. I arranged to spend a day with a teacher friend of mine in her Grade

4 class, and I knew within an hour that I had found my new career. A very valuable book as you create your new life!

Another excellent book by Barbara Sher is *Live the Life You Love: In Ten Easy Step-By Step Lessons* (DTP, 1997). This book is intended as a follow up to *I Could Do Anything If I Only Knew What It Was*, and helps you define your dreams, get rid of things in your life that are holding you back, and get a live that you truly love and that fits you perfectly. Also highly recommended!

WEB SITES

There are a lot of Internet sites on being childfree. A lot of them, however, are quite anti-child. While some of them do also contain helpful information, they might be too difficult for you to read in the early stages of being childfree. If you wish to find some of these web sites, simply type 'childfree' into any search engine. I will list a few of my favourite sites, however.

About.com's Living Childfree After Infertility area (http://infertility.about. com/library/rti/blchildfree.htm) does have some interesting and useful information. I have noticed a tendency to slip into being child*less* rather than child*free* among some of the regular posters in this area; do be careful and read with an open mind.

The 'childfree-by-choice pages', at http://www.childfree.net, are slightly more anti-child. However, they do have some very valuable information. In particular, click on the "Potpourri" link, and find the "Evaluation", which helps you decide what is motivating you to have children. This site also has a list of well-known people who are childfree, which can be interesting, as well as a well-written discussion of whether it is selfish to remain childfree.

"Turtle's Childfree Pages" (http://www.fred.net/turtle/kids/kids1.html) are quite militantly anti-child. If you feel able to handle this, however, there is some wonderful information here, and a message board.

I have recently found a very interesting online article at http://www.olist.com/ essays/text/ray/shame_children.html, called "The Shame of Not Wanting Children". The author, Carolyn Ray, presents a very reasoned discussion of living childfree, and there is some excellent information included in the article.

"The Child-Free Zone" in Australia (http://www.childfree.com.au/) is also a very useful site. It has a lot of information, as well as being a selling site for a book called "Child-Free Zone".

Finally, I have my own web site. Located at http://www.childfree.ca, it is called "Choosing to be Childfree". My site includes details of how I became childfree, links to additional information, and is also the home page of my mailing list. If the links to any of the information that I have provided here change, I will post the updated information on my site.

INTERNET MAILING LISTS

There are quite a few Internet mailing lists dealing with being infertile, and some that *say* that they are about becoming childfree after infertility. Unfortunately, most of them actually seem to slip into spending years being sad about being infertile rather than moving on into being childfree. I tried out several of this mailing lists as I moved from being childless to childfree, and I cannot recommend any of them because of this. Some people, however, have found some of these groups to be very helpful. My suggestion, if you are interested, is to choose a group, and subscribe for a while. If you find that the tone of the group is pulling you down rather than helping you become childfree, unsubscribe.

I have my own mailing list, which I started because I could not find the support group I needed. Created in 1999, I currently have over two hundred group members! Not everyone posts regularly, of course, and the list has its quiet times. Still, it is a very supportive group of people, and friendly to those who are coming to the childfree lifestyle after infertility. (I take an active role in moderating the list, and do not permit topics to continue if they are excessively child hating or rude.) The list is hosted at Yahoo!, and can be found at http://groups.yahoo.com/group/CF_and_like_kids/

The 'main childfree list' can be found at http://www.childfree.net/list.html. This list can be *very* child hating. It is the first resource that I found when I first began to consider being childfree, and I am grateful to it for that. However, I began to be far more negative about children than I really wanted to be, so I am no longer a member.

NO KIDDING! SOCIAL GROUP

No Kidding! provides social activities for adults without children. It is not a political or lobby group; it is simply a way to meet other childfree adults and enjoy their company. The first chapter is in Vancouver, British Columbia, and there are no chapters all over the world. Their web site is http://www.nokidding.net/. My web site hosts the pages of the Toronto, Ontario chapter.

Appendix B

Stories

The following stories are reproduced here exactly as they were originally sent to me. I have done a *small* amount of editing for grammar, and replaced abbreviations with the full words, but the stories are unchanged. These women very kindly gave me permission to include their full stories, in the hopes that they might be helpful. I have also included my own story, extracted from my web site.

Cathy's story

I was married young, and my husband and I didn't start trying till we'd been married 7 years. We tried naturally for a while, and eventually learned we had problems. My husband did some sperm testing, with mixed results, sometimes low motility, other times fairly normal. I did years of temperature charts, 2 hysterosalpingograms, 2 laparoscopies, ultrasound, and many months of Clomid and progesterone. I had 3 infertility doctors, but none could find any definitive problem.

On a break from Clomid in 1995, I did get pregnant. It was the happiest time of my life. The joy of telling my husband, and each person in turn, (my dreams for years) the inclusion in "the mommy club", the pure joy of that short time. I lost my baby at 8 weeks. I was devastated.

By 1990, I was so emotionally rung out from the infertility roller coaster, that I just couldn't take the pain (and loss) each month any more. I stopped seeing my doctor very abruptly (I never got the results of my last test with her).

I know my husband isn't completely in agreement with me, but he did little in this battle, while I fought to the very edge at times. I know many of my friends and family still don't understand why I've "given up", and they still make some comments.

I was *unbelievably* lonely, until I typed "childfree" into the Internet. I found a group of people who were happy to be CF, and didn't fit in, but they did tell me about the group I'm in now. It is a wonderful group of women, whose support I don't know how I'd get along without. I cherish them.

(Heather's note: check Appendix A for information on Internet groups for the childfree after infertility.)

ELLEN'S STORY

In March of 1983, a Nurse Practitioner giving me a routine pelvic examination announced, "You're at least eight weeks pregnant." This came as a surprise to me, since I faithfully took a birth control pill every morning.

I immediately made an appointment with a gynecologist, who turned out to be the doctor who would guide me through the year-long process of diagnosing my infertility and presenting me with options to deal with it.

What the Nurse Practitioner believed was an enlarged womb actually was a very large cyst on my left ovary. In April, 1983, I had it surgically removed. A biopsy revealed an extremely small amount of cancer at the center of the ovary. However, this wasn't the emotionally painful diagnosis. That came moments later when my gynecologist informed me that I had massive fibroids and endometriosis.

"I don't think you're fertile or ever have been fertile," he said, "and if you want to have children, I suggest we surgically remove as much of the fibroids and endometriosis as possible and that you try to get pregnant immediately." I was 21 years old.

Although I was married, so having a child seem like a logical "next step," I realized after twelve months of soul-searching that I was not ready to take on the responsibility of a child. Had I had to make this decision at age 30, or even 25, perhaps I would have chosen differently, but at age 21 I knew with certainty that I did not want to bring a child into the world without being completely ready emotionally and, frankly, financially. (I have fairly strong feelings about establishing a career and financial base for the household before bringing children into the picture.)

In addition, my husband was divorced, with a young daughter, and his ex-wife had absconded with the child. (It took us over a decade to find her, which is another story!) He had always only wanted one child. In fact, six years before we met, he'd had a vasectomy. (Though I knew this when I married him, I'd hoped to perhaps persuade him to have it reversed. A childish notion, since in those days vasectomies were pretty definitely permanent.)

I was in extreme physical pain. I could barely sit down in a chair comfortably. My gynecologist again told me he didn't believe I was fertile. Even if I did attempt to get pregnant, he couldn't guarantee success. (And at that time, infertility treatments were not yet very advanced. In vitro fertilization was barely an option—and an expensive one, at that.)

In April, 1984, at age 22, I had my right ovary and uterus surgically removed. Because I was so young, my gynecologist wisely recommended counseling for me to explore my feelings about my infertility. I attended counseling for about a year and, to my surprise, realized I didn't feel particularly sad about my situation. I concluded that I had been given a rare opportunity: to pursue a "self-centered" life without the burden of children. I had the opportunity to travel, to aggressively pursue career options, to salt away money for my own benefit instead of having to spend it on my children's needs.

Perhaps it helped that I had an intimate role model for this type of lifestyle. My mother's brother and his wife were infertile and opted to live child-free. As we were a close-knit family when I was a child, I got to know a happy, well-adjusted childless couple. I saw the benefits they enjoyed from their lifestyle and how they took joy from their interactions with their nieces and nephews. I resolved to do the same.

In another stroke of wisdom, my gynecologist had warned me that my biological clock did not know I'd had a hysterectomy and might ratchet up its ticking as I entered my thirties. Boy, was he right! The most remorse I've felt over the situation occurred nearly 15 years after my hysterectomy. Between ages 30 and 35, I felt strong yearnings for a child. I talked with my husband at length about the possibility of adopting a child (or two). My sister even offered to bear a child for us, in what I consider the most selfless offer I've ever experienced. However, my husband stood firm in his resolve not to have more children. He made rational arguments to me ("We're not in a financial position to adopt") to emotional ones ("Honey, you've told me many times how happy and comfortable you are being childfree. Has that really changed, or are you just feeling overwhelmed by your biological urge?") By age 36, the urge had largely passed. For a variety of reasons, I'm glad my husband talked me out of having a child.

Now, at age 40, I take great joy in tending my two step-grandchildren and my infant nephew. Through expressing my maternal side in this way, I have learned that I would have made a great mother. This knowledge fills me with both relief and a tinge of sadness/regret. On the one hand, it's nice to know I could have succeeded as a mother (I believe now I always had hidden doubts about that), but on the other hand it makes me feel sad about what might have been.

Thus, at this point in the journey (and make no mistake, infertility and/or child-freedom is a lifelong journey; it doesn't simply end when the decision is made to pursue the lifestyle), I am very comfortable with my decision to remain childfree, though this comfortability harbors the slightest bit of melancholy. Instead of dwelling on any of the negative aspects of childfreedom, I choose to focus on all the positives. Denial? I don't think so. Rather, I think it represents a healthy way to deal with the issue. "There's no sense crying over spilt milk."

Good luck with your book. I think it's a much-needed work as our society evolves into a children-by-choice phase instead of a children-as-expected phase.

EMMA'S STORY

After nearly a year of trying to conceive with no success, I sought out advice from my gynecologist during my yearly check-up. He performed some preliminary tests on both my husband and myself. He then referred us to a fertility specialist. It was incredibly frustrating because it took several months to have our initial visit with our reproductive endocrinologist. We finally got to see our doctor. That was more than a year ago. I have tried a variety of fertility drugs, had several intra-uterine inseminations, and had surgery. After about ten or eleven cycles with no success, I had laparoscopic surgery this past summer. Stage 3 endometriosis was found and removed. I felt really hopeful that that might have been the blocker that was keeping us from having a family. However, the past two cycles have been miserable failures where my body didn't even get to the stage of ovulation so we couldn't even attempt an insemination.

This has been a really difficult emotional struggle. The cycle of hope and disappointment has been like a roller coaster ride. Although, so far, I don't dare get off in case that the opportunity of becoming pregnant is waiting just around the next turn or corkscrew or over the next hill. On top of that, having so many hormones because of the medications, I am never quite sure the extent that my feelings are authentic and the amount that the medication is affecting me.

Luckily, my husband and I have been in this thing together. We've managed to support and comfort each other. Now I feel like our journey on this quest is nearing the end. We kind of set an amount of attempts we would try after the surgery. Because of expense of procedure and lack of insurance coverage, it isn't feasible for us to pursue in-vitro fertilization. I keep trying to come to terms with the idea of letting go of trying.

We have talked about the ideas of adopting and living childfree. We continue to go back and forth on the issue. Ultimately we have to ask ourselves, will we regret not having kids in the future. I guess we are still working on our answer to that question.

KATHERINE'S STORY

Ten years ago, if someone had asked me what I where I was going to be in the next ten years, I would have answered "marriage and a family with two or three children."

I would not have thought of any other option. After all, isn't that what women did?

That's what the women in my family did. I might have felt differently if I had had one childfree relative who I admired, but I didn't.

I had my life planned, or so I thought.

I never really thought seriously enough about what I wanted to do for a career, as I figured that whatever career I chose would be put on the backburner once I got married and had children.

In 1987, I got my degree in Advertising with a minor in Psychology. After graduation, I ended up doing a two-year stint at a Manhattan based firm as a buyer for television infomercial time.

Following that, I took a job for a local newspaper selling advertising space. It wasn't what I truly wanted to do, but I also thought that I wouldn't be there any longer than 3-4 years. I thought once I got married and the baby came that I would not longer be in that position. I really looked forward to being a stay-at-home mom. After all, that is what my mother did for many years.

The script was written. All I had to do was play the part.

I never considered the fact that I didn't really enjoy being around children and that toddlers grated against my nerves. I distinctly remember worrying about how I would deal with the problem of a messy, screechy toddler and concluding that everything would fall in place once I had my own.

My husband and I got married in May of 1994 and began trying to conceive that following January. We both wanted to start right away, as we were both "older". I was 30 and he was 41. I had gone to the doctor who told me that he could not foresee any problems. I thought that meant it would take no longer than three months.

It turned into a countdown. It wasn't just a countdown toward the conception of a child, but a countdown of a different kind—the leaving of my job! For once, I could see the light at the end of the tunnel.

I had visions of me home with the baby or at the mall with a stroller playing Susie Homemaker. The Toddler Issue still nagged at me, although it was something I chose to ignore.

Months passed by without conception. "What could possibly be wrong?" I thought as I saw everyone around me getting pregnant and having babies. I tried not to think about it. Sometimes I thought about it too much.

Lovemaking became somewhat of a chore. I remember lying in bed with my feet straight up in the air and my back supported by my hands. I maintained this position for 20 minutes or more after each intercourse.

With each passing month and each onset of a new period, I grew increasingly depressed. Why was I unable to do something so simple as to get pregnant? Teenagers did it all the time!

I began to go out less and less. I no longer felt "up to" the strains of an active social life. I did not want to be questioned by well-meaning acquaintances. I just wanted to be left alone.

During this time, I was trying to get my husband to go for tests. After all, it was much easier to test a man than it was for a woman. He always found some excuse as to why he couldn't. I later found out that he didn't want either of us to carry the burden of responsibility. According to him, ignorance was bliss.

Of course, I took the burden onto myself anyway and one day while he and I were at the kitchen table, I asked him point-blank, "What would you do if we didn't have children?"

His response? "Well, then we wouldn't have children."

"Yeah, but what would you do if we didn't have children?"

"I don't understand the question. We just wouldn't have children!"

Exasperated and rolling my eyes, I blurted, "I'm asking if you would leave me if we weren't able to have children. I would understand if you wanted to leave me, but tell me now because I have to know."

He sat there, dumbfounded.

"But I married you because I loved you, not because I wanted a child. If we have children, great, but I wouldn't leave you because we couldn't have children. Besides, what makes you think it is your fault anyway?"

I later asked him if, hypothetically, it was my fault and if we had that knowledge before we got married would he still have married me. He answered that he did not know. I knew it was an unfair question, given the change in the dynamics of the situation, but I need to ask anyway.

What followed was a serious depression. I also made a bad business decision that I don't think I would have made were it not for the baby issue.

I was desperate. I began to realize that I might never have a baby and that I needed another way out. Friends of ours introduced us to a multi-level marketing business that looked promising. Initially, I began to see the light at the end of the tunnel and began to work towards financial freedom. What happened was quite different. I was spinning my wheels and getting nowhere fast. I sunk deeper and deeper into depression.

I still never gave up on the baby. I remember for each and every period that came, I would cry my eyes out. What was something that was so easy for others so difficult for me? What had I done to deserve this?

During this time, we never saw any fertility specialist. We could never get past the sperm testing and no one would speak with us unless the man was tested first.

Then it hit me. I'm not sure of when it hit me. That was a shame, as I would have loved to know a date.

I remember where I was though. I know exactly at what corner and at what light I was sitting. I was in my now defunct 1990 Nissan Sentra four-door sedan when this revelation hit. It was mid-morning on a winter's day, probably in February of 1997.

I heard a voice inside my head tell me, "You're too young to be feeling this way. You know that whether or not you conceive does not make any difference in the kind of woman you are. How much longer are you going to let this ruin your days?"

That was it. I never looked back. Never felt bad or guilty. It was as if someone had turned on a light. No more pain and no more crying.

I had my life back again.

In 1998, I had gone to my gynecologist complaining about severe pain. My mother had a history of endometriosis, so I thought I might too. My doctor at the time suggested I might want to see a fertility doctor.

Was I still interested in having a baby? By now I wasn't sure. After all, my life seemed set and we had a pattern. I wasn't sure whether or not I wanted such a drastic change. I agreed because I thought I might find out what was wrong.

The surgery revealed a large amount of endometriosis as well as fibroids, all of which she removed.

At the follow-up, she asked us if we wanted to pursue fertility treatments and we told her that we would have to think about it.

My husband and I discussed it, and we both decided that it was not worth the emotional or physical toll. It wasn't worth the anguish. We had the lives that we wanted and it didn't seem as important to have children. We had each other.

People ask why we don't adopt. Adoption was not the right choice for us. Neither my husband nor I could imagine raising another couple's child. We wanted a child that we would have created together, beginning from one cell created from a bond of perfect love and perfect trust. An adopted child is a human being, with thoughts, feelings, and emotions. Wouldn't it be terrible if that child felt that they were "second best?" No, we could not do that to another human being.

People ask me what will happen when I get older. I tell them I will age and eventually die.

People ask if I worry about who will take care of me when I am no longer able to take care of myself. I tell them that nursing homes are filled with people with children, people who wait day after day for their children to visit.

A close friend of mine is a nursing home administrator who delivered some shocking news to me one day. She said that she couldn't count the times that she is told my residents' children not to be notified unless their parent(s) are dead.

She said more often than not, it is the friends who sign people into the facility and it is the friends who visit most often.

Being childfree has opened up a lifestyle to me that I never knew possible. While my friends are worried about their children and are stuck at home, my husband and I are out enjoying active social lives and cultivating friendships. We are living outside the box and we like it that way.

Who would have thought that this would be a choice?

TABITHA'S STORY

Note: I don't know if I am happy about not having a child, but at this time I am not sad.

We first conceived just before we married when we were trying to prevent it. At ten weeks I started spotting and had to have a dilatation and curettage. We were disappointed, but had a lot of hope for future children in our marriage; besides, this happens to a lot of people who are perfectly healthy and reproductively sound.

I went on birth control for the next year so we could spend that time adjusting to our new lives together, and then we decided to go off the pill and just let nature take its course.

After about a year without any pregnancy we bought the thermometer and chart and arranged our love making around the graph. Since we had already conceived once we didn't think we would need a doctor's help so we stuck with the charting and timing for a year.

At this point it was time to admit that we needed help and went to a reproductive endocrinologist. I went in with the attitude that I won't take any drugs; we're just going to find out what is wrong and see if we can get it fixed. After sperm analysis, a post coital test, all kinds of blood tests, and the one where they inject dye into your uterus and watch it on the x-ray, we looked in perfect reproductive health.

The most logical next step was Clomid with intra-uterine insemination, so we gave it a try. The cycle was unsuccessful and we were now in a busy unpredictable season with our business so we had to postpone further treatment for a few months.

About three months after the Clomid cycle we learned that we were pregnant again. We were so excited (besides, we already had our miscarriage) that we bought nursery furniture and a couple of maternity outfits, but we guarded this news and kept it to ourselves just in case.

Three weeks later ultrasounds revealed that the fetus was not growing. Another dilatation and curettage was performed the following week. After the initial disappointment we were hopeful, because this time they were going to run a battery of tests on the fetus to try to find out why it didn't survive. The results came back showing XXX instead of XX; I think this is called triploid something. In a way this was a relief because they think this is a common problem that happens but has nothing to do with either parent, just a "fluke" of nature.

So we gave the fertility treatments another rest to recoup emotionally and maybe conceive on our own again. No luck, so we tried three more cycles of the Clomid with intra-uterine insemination without success. By this time we were both feeling like we were being punished for having premarital sex or something. Aren't we good enough to have children? Won't we be good parents?

The next step was a huge one for me, a SOURCE cycle. Injectables with intra-uterine insemination, followed by progesterone suppositories. The morning I had to go in for a baseline ultrasound I cried in my husband's arms. I did not want to stick needles in myself and I did not want seven babies. Fortunately I had a cyst and would have to wait until the next cycle. I was relieved and in that month I was able to come to terms with what I had to do.

I was amazed at how easy the injections were and got to where I looked forward to taking them since I knew they were going to help me have a baby. The worst one was the HCG that my husband had to give me in my hip. We were both very nervous about it. He was so afraid of hurting my and I still don't know what I was afraid of, but my fear was strong enough that I iced the injection site for twenty minutes, I turned my head away, closed my eyes, and I even plugged my ears. I didn't feel a thing. My husband was white as a sheet and quite shaky when it was over, but he did very well.

We must have done it right, because we were pregnant again. This time we guarded our emotions more than ever. We didn't buy anything and I wouldn't let myself read any further in my pregnancy book than where I was in my term.

This time the baby did grow between the 1st & 2nd ultrasound but it wasn't as large as most pregnancies at that stage. Our doctor said that we still had a chance but to prepare ourselves for another miscarriage.

That weekend we had to drive to a wedding 6 hours away so our reproductive endocrinologist gave us the name and phone number of another reproductive endocrinologist in that area just in case we needed it. The wedding was beautiful and everybody was having a great time while I pretended to. I refused to dance and made numerous trips to the restroom to see if I started spotting. During the entire weekend I kept thinking that this couple (who're very dear to us) were going to have a baby before us and we've been trying for over six years.

On Monday another ultrasound showed no growth and we scheduled another dilatation and curettage for that same week. This time the procedure was extremely painful. We were in the doctor's office for about four hours before I could leave. While I was lying on the table in so much pain that I was shaking uncontrollably I kept thinking that I must be too much of a wimp to have a baby and maybe that's why I can't.

This fetus was tested as well and had the same problem as the last one. This concerned our reproductive endocrinologist enough that he sent us to a genetic counselor. They pretty much told us that either we were struck by lightning twice or there could be something wrong with our eggs or sperm. Basically we were still at square one.

At this point we started thinking about my two retarded brothers and checked into that. We don't know why they are retarded, but they were suspicious of Fragile X so I was tested for that. Negative. There were really no other tests to put them through since they had been through it all ten years prior with my other older sister and brother when they were having children.

Somewhere in here (about four weeks after the wedding we attended) I got an email from the happy couple, they're pregnant! And due just one month after our due date would have been (December 18). We did not celebrate Christmas last year; I just cried my way through December. And I started seeing a psychologist in January.

Now that we'd done all the checking that the reproductive endocrinologists could think of to do, we tried three more SOURCE cycles, always trying to fine tune and trying different gonadotropins. By the last cycle, we went to progesterone injections since the suppositories caused spotting. These injections also had to be given by my husband and he got very good at it but he'd always shiver after each one. We also got pretty relaxed with them; he'd be in his recliner and I'd bring the prepared needle and stand in front of him watching TV. We were beginning to think this isn't so bad when one time I bled when he removed the needle. He had to run to the bathroom to vomit. The last two injections I gave to myself in the thigh.

Not pregnant again. This was March of this year.

We talked to our reproductive endocrinologist and I talked with my psychologist trying to decide if we want to try in-vitro fertilization and if we do, do we want to use donor eggs (maybe there is something wrong with me that is related to my brothers); or do we want to adopt. We could not come to a conclusion so we decided not to do anything.

We are pretending that we decided to live childfree. I finally bought the car I wanted (we don't have insurance that covers infertility treatments), we're planning two vacations (the first ones we'll take in over three years), and we bought a DVD player. We had been so scared to spend any money.

Now it is mid-July and life feels pretty good. Our sex life is beginning to be fun again and we're able to plan for our future.

A couple of months ago we watched a movie about a football player who was in an auto accident and was left paralyzed. By the end of the movie I felt like I knew exactly what he was going through. I told my husband that I felt like that kid; I have to accept that I can't have children and figure out how to get on with my life and be happy with the way I am.

I'm not ready to say that I won't go back to treatment, but right now it doesn't look very appealing. I know what pain we will be facing if we go back.

I still get a little sad when I see a newborn, but I've found that I don't enjoy being around older children and I have to smile to myself when I see frustrated parents trying to correct their children in public, knowing that I won't have to suffer that embarrassment and hassle.

WENDY'S STORY

I went through fertility therapy in my early thirties. No one was ever able to determine why I couldn't become pregnant. Though not an extensive effort, I found the tests and doctors' visits and questions to be invasive, demeaning, and embarrassing. The process itself made me feel like a sort of invalid, though I had never felt that way before I started it.

I was a strong, healthy, lively young woman who turned into an emotional basket case due to the infertility process. I cried a great deal. I took Clomid and visited specialists for over a year. When the doctor suggested Pergonal injections, I feared multiple births, and gave it up.

In retrospect, I think I may have just wanted to fulfill society's (and my parents') expectations of me. I am now 52, about to retire from public school teaching/counseling, still married to the same man after 27.5 years, and completely contented to be childfree.

HEATHER'S STORY

The following is taken from my web site, and describes what my infertility experience was like.

My husband and I married in 1995, while we still had one year of university left, so children weren't a real question then. (Although I did harbour secret thoughts of having a honeymoon baby!!)

Once we'd graduated and started working, though, I started feeling like something was missing, and that we needed a baby. My husband, smart man that he is, knew he wasn't yet ready, and told me so. I most definitely did NOT want to have a baby without him being ready, and I'm not big on pushing him to do things (at least, not things that are that important!), so we waited, mostly patiently. (I'm not exactly known for my patience, but I tried!!)

Late 1997, my husband decided he was ready, pending a few small issues. (Such as checking the budget to make sure we could live on his salary—I believe that one person should stay home with the kids, and since I made less money, it was going to be me!) Once those issues were resolved, we started trying in November 1997.

We were convinced, Christmas 1997, that we'd succeeded. (After all, we're both young and healthy, so no worries!) Despite the lack of a positive pregnancy test, we nearly told our families at Christmas. Happily, we didn't, because we were wrong.

And continued to be wrong, until May 1998. By this time, we'd been nearly 6 months, and nothing seemed to be happening. I was doing all of the temperature charting stuff to decide when I was fertile, and my charts looked more like random squiggles than anything resembling a normal pattern. I just kept thinking I was doing it wrong (question: how does one take one's temperature wrong?)

So, in May, I went to my doctor. She said, "Oh, here, take these pills; I have a few girls who have trouble getting pregnant, and these are really mild but they'll get things going." Anyone ever heard of Clomid?? They're NOT that mild, and they don't always get things going, if you have an underlying medical condition. But, hey, we don't really need to worry about investigating the problem, right, just pop some pills! (In the immortal words of Homer J. Simpson: "In case you can't tell, I'm being sarcastic.")

So, poor naive Heather goes off and takes the pills. One bright side, I'm not so worried about menopause now that I've experienced hot flashes! But still, no pregnancy.

In the second month of the pills, we believe I did in fact get pregnant, but miscarried two weeks later. (The specialist I dealt with later disputes this, because "women can have a weird period and not realize it's not really anything different". Why yes, it WAS a male doctor. :)

After three months of the pills, my doctor said, "Gee, I dunno…maybe you should see a specialist." So I did that. He ordered a 'test' on my husband, which came back normal. After looking at me for a minute, he concluded I probably had polycystic ovarian syndrome, a condition that causes the ovaries not to release eggs. (Of course, if these same ovaries are stimulated by Clomid, they just try and fail to release MORE eggs—not exactly successful!)

The doctor scheduled a laparoscopy (exploratory surgery through the belly button) to confirm his diagnosis—confirmed!

But before the surgery happened, I had basically fallen apart. I was reduced to crying at any and all baby-related commercials (and have you ever noticed just how bloody many of those there are??), I could barely control myself from smacking pregnant women because they'd achieved what I wanted, and if I saw one doing something 'bad' (like, oh, eating a cookie), I wanted to scream at her. Not an emotionally balanced person, let's just say.

I finally snapped one day a few weeks before the laparoscopy was going to be done. My husband and I were at the mall, and two women walked by with babies. I burst into tears, and had to be taken out of the mall and driven home, crying all the way. We got home, and I cuddled up with our cats and cried some more. Eventually, I started thinking about why we were doing this, and about whether it was what I wanted.

When I'm trying to make a decision, I often imagine myself deciding first one way, then the other, and see which way feels right. So I thought, "I'm not going to try for a baby anymore." I felt such a strong sense of peace and 'rightness'; when I tried to imagine trying again, I simply couldn't do it. I told my husband, "I don't want to do this anymore," and he agreed.

We had certainly talked a great deal before about when we should have children, how we would raise them, and what sorts of things we wanted to have in place before we had them. However, we had spent no time discussing or considering whether we actually *wanted* children—we just assumed that we did.

Once it became obvious that it wasn't going to be as easy for us as it 'should have been', we began to take the time to do what we should really have done earlier—decide whether we wanted a child, not just where we would fit one into our lives. (Or, perhaps more accurately, change our lives to suit one.)

We discovered that I was expecting having a child to make me feel like an adult, like a "grown-up". I was in my late twenties, but I didn't feel grown-up, despite owning a house, two cars, holding down a great job, etc. (Interestingly, I feel MUCH more 'grown-up' now that we've made this decision.) My husband, on the other hand, basically wanted a child because I did. (He does also like children, to a degree—the quiet well-behaved (mythical!) ones.)

Would we have made good parents? Probably. Did we have any remotely good reason for having a child? Not even close.

I went through with the surgery, because I did want to know what was wrong. After the surgery, the doctor suggested a year of a special birth control pill that can help to treat the condition, and we agreed wholeheartedly. That year ended September 1999, and there is NO way that we will be going back to trying for a baby. Our lives just seem better now; we're infinitely less stressed and less in pain. We feel less and less like we've missed out on something and more and more like we've dodged a bullet.

APPENDIX C

References

In Chapter 6, I referred to several scientific studies of what happens to the child-free as they age. Here are the references for those studies.

Connidis, I. A., & McMullin, J. A. "To have or have not: Parental status and the subjective well-being of older men and women." *The Gerontologist* 33 (1993): 630-636.

Mueller, K.A., & Yoder, J.D. "Stigmatization of non-normative family size status." *Sex Roles* 41 (1999): 901-919.

Zhang, Z., & Hayward, M.D. "Childlessness and the psychological well-being of older persons." *The Journals of Gerontology* 56B (2001): S311-S320.

0-595-27438-2

Made in the USA
Lexington, KY
13 February 2019